KENTUCKY CRONE
GUIDE TO ESSENTIAL OILS
AND OTHER TIPS FROM SOUTHERN GRANNIES

ISBN-13: 978-1535034432
ISBN-10: 1535034432

PUBLISHERS NOTE

NOTICE OF RIGHTS

DISCLAIMER

Lord o' mercy.

My nephew says I have to state the following:

> "This information is for reference purposes only.
>
> Statements are not intended as a substitute for professional healthcare nor meant to diagnose, treat, cure, or prevent medical conditions or disease.
>
> Every illness or injury requires supervision by a medical doctor or alternative medicine practitioner."
> —*fancy pants lawyer*

Bless your pea-picking little heart.

CONTENTS

INTRO

Meemaw Crone starts each day puttering through the hills of Kentucky gathering items for her crafts. All Kentucky Crone serums are manufactured in Kentucky, however, the ingredients come from many places. Believing the natural, old ways are best, Meemaw only uses organic carrier oils, and pharmaceutical grade essential oils.

Money is tight, so Meemaw encourages you to order samples from manufacturers when available. Meemaw was shocked to see the cost of serums made with quality ingredients. Money isn't everything, but it sure keeps the kids in touch.

Kentucky Crone could easily skimp on materials, using non-pharmaceutical grade oil, or non-organic products, but what would be the point?

Plenty of substandard serums are available on the market. If you don't care what you put on your skin, save yourself some money.

You can create your own serums with a little experimentation, and that is why Meemaw made this guide.

Hard work never hurt anybody, so get your ducks lined up in a row and make hay while the sun shines.

A mad stone is a hairball taken from the stomach of a sheep. Boiled and applied to an animal bite, it is said to draw out rabies.
—Mommie O'Noggie

Put ambeer (tobacco juice) on a wasp sting to draw out the poison. —Granny Cecile

HISTORY AND TRADITION

Essential oil, the concentrated aromatic essence from a plant, could be called the plant's psyche. Essential oil is sometimes called the soul of an aromatic plant. This life-force substance is more thin and watery than oily, making the name somewhat of a misnomer. Consistency aside, essences are highly concentrated and extremely volatile, often containing hundreds of organic components.

Essential oils include hormones, vitamins, and chemicals needed to perform plant functions. A flower's essence attracts insects for pollination. In a shrub or tree, the essential oil becomes resin to heal wounds from severe weather damage. Essential oil regulates the water content in a plant and prevents evaporation. Or, a plant might produce chemicals to deter predators and warn other plants and trees. Often a plant produces a toxic substance against bacteria, virus or fungus. The essential oils of these highly complex organisms are one of nature's gifts to human beings. They freshen the atmosphere, enrich the food, and heal whatever ails the body, mind or spirit.

Essential oils have been used for thousands of years in the art and science of aromatherapy. Chinese ruler Shen Nung is credited with discovering the medicinal properties of plants and writing the first herbal catalog of more than 200 botanicals, *Pen Tsao* (c. 2700-3000 BC). Archaeologists continually find evidence of therapeutic uses for essential oils in the civilizations of ancient China, India, and the Middle East. Ayurveda, traditional Hindu medicine practiced throughout the world, utilizes herbal treatment with origins in the 2nd millennium BC.

Ancient Egyptians used incense, infusions, ointments and resins for various religious ceremonies. Queen Cleopatra kept hundreds of flowers and used their essences to perfume her body and surroundings. Terracotta urns filled with aromatic oils accompanied Pharaohs to the afterlife. Roman soldiers treated wounds with honey and myrrh and emperors and scholars relaxed in legendary perfumed baths. The Old and New Testaments of the Bible contain detailed recipes using aromatic compounds.

Widespread use of essential oils throughout Europe flourished with the invention of glass distillation methods and the microscope, and the discovery of new trade routes. These developments ushered in extraction of essential oil from plants like French Rosemary, Italian Chamomile, and Lavender from England. Queen Elizabeth I used an abundant supply of English Lavender oil throughout her life, a practice continued by Queen Victoria during her entire 64-year reign. The tradition was upheld in the latter 20th century by Diana, Princess of Wales, who was often photographed travelling between Kensington Palace and her aromatherapist's office.

Modern aromatherapy was born in the early 20th century when Rene-Maurice Gattefosse, a French chemist working for a prominent perfumer, accidentally set his arm on fire in the laboratory. He thrust it into the nearest vat of cold liquid, which happened to be Lavender oil, and felt immediate relief. Previous chemical burns had caused severe pain, redness, blisters, and scarring. Surprisingly, this burn healed quickly with minimal pain and no scarring. Gattefosse coined the word *aromatherapie* to describe his healing experience. He spent the rest of his life researching the health benefits of essential oils and published his findings in the 1937 landmark book *Aromatherapy*. It was translated into English in 1993 and the 2nd edition is still in print, 70 years later.

French physician Jean Valnet continued the work of Gattefosse during World War II, using essential oils to successfully treat wounded soldiers with gangrene, reducing the need for amputation. His book, *The Practice of Aromatherapy*, popularized aromatherapy for medical and psychiatric use throughout France in the 1960s.

In 1962, Marguerite Maury published findings which heralded the cosmetic benefits of essential oils. The first English language book, *The Art of*

Aromatherapy by Robert Tisserand (1977) introduced the benefits of aromatherapy coupled with massage, and advanced the practice in the United Kingdom and the United States.

The New Age movement latched onto aromatherapy soon after. A burgeoning of holistic, natural medicine since the 1980s has provided a comfortable environment for aromatherapy.

Aromatherapy benefits are achieved through two pathways—inhalation, or topical application. Do not ingest essential oils. They are rarely suggested for internal use even under a licensed medical practitioner's direction.

Inhaling an essential oil increases brain frequency, balances right and left brain activities, and signals the release of hormones to specific areas of the body. Applied to the skin, essential oils enter the bloodstream and draw to specific body parts that need healing. One oil might be effective with muscle tissue, another might be drawn toward bone marrow.

HOW DO I USE ESSENTIAL OILS?

Depending on your needs, you should carefully choose which essential oils are best for you. Essential oils can be inhaled as a mist in the air, smelled from a bottle or locket, rubbed into the joints or skin diluted with carrier oils, or as a diluted topical cream for skin breakouts.

Most mood enhancing essential oils combat mental fatigue, stress, and anxiety. For problems with the skin, use essential oils that help with rashes, infections, or acne problems. It is important to use the proper essential oil or you may find yourself frustrated from no effect.

Before choosing an essential oil, research and read articles related to several essential oils. Some essential oils are better as mood enhancers. If you suffer from depression or low self-esteem, certain essential oils will lift your spirits and increase your mood to be more active during the day. Ask a professional or qualified consultant to help you choose which essential oil will help your condition with the best efficiency.

After you choose an essential oil it is important to test it before using it. Essential oils should never be applied without testing a small area of the skin. Never use essential oils without first diluting the extract. Essential oils are potent, so using them on the skin without diluting can cause a rash or burn.

To patch test, dilute a small drop in a few milliliters of vegetable oil. Spread the essential oil cream on a small area of your skin and observe for twenty-four hours. If your skin becomes irritated or red, then you may be allergic to that specific oil. Use this method even before burning essential oils for aromatherapy.

After checking for allergies, it is time to use the essential oils. There are several different methods. Below is a list of ways to inhale or apply the essential oils for the different therapeutic effects.

DIFFUSER

A diffuser will allow you to inhale the essential oils. Put a few drops of essential oils into the diffuser with water. Some essential oils can be used with heat, so make sure to read the directions. A diffuser will evaporate the essential oils into the air, and most come with a timer for use while sleeping. Feel free to experiment with mixing oils in different combinations.

DRY EVAPORATION

Dry evaporation is a simple way to inhale the essential oils. Place a few drops on a cotton swab or tissue and allow it to evaporate into the air. If you need a quick, strong scent, inhale the fragrance from the bottle. For a less potent effect, allow the essential oils to evaporate on the tissue or cotton and leave it near where you will remain for about an hour.

STEAM

Steam is a simple way to inhale the essential oil aroma. Place a few drops into a steaming bowl of water. The oils will quickly vaporize into the air. Place a towel over your head and place your head close to the steam and inhale. The fresh fragrance will penetrate your senses and help you feel refreshed.

If you can't afford health insurance, you can always rely on the placebo effect.
—Meemaw Crone

PROPER WAYS TO APPLY ESSENTIAL OILS

Although essential oils are a mild, natural way to help fight off mental fatigue, stress, sore muscles, and other physical conditions, they are potent and need proper application. After you have bought the perfect essential oils for your condition, it is important to know how to apply them. If used without proper direction, they can have a negative affect or cause harm to the skin or nasal passages.

Used undiluted on the skin, essential oils can sometimes leave a rash or a burn, leaving painful sores. Diluting the essential oils in cream or non-greasy oil will keep it from damaging your skin.

Spreading essential oils directly on the skin can cause an overdose. Essential oils absorb into skin quickly. If the oil that you are applying isn't diluted, it can also cause a skin breakout. Also avoid sun overexposure, especially if you've accidentally applied too much. Sun exposure can lead to adverse reactions.

Even though essential oils are naturally occurring extracts from plants and trees, they are also powerful therapeutic agents. It is important to keep them out of the reach of children. Spreading essential oils undiluted onto a child's skin can be dangerous. If ingested, it can be lethal to a child and the caretaker should contact emergency medical personnel immediately.

When applying essential oils be sure to keep it away from your eyes, nose, ears, and any mucous membranes. The oils should never be ingested or allowed to enter the internal body. Keeping the essential oils away from openings on your body can ensure your overall health and remove the possibility of an overdose. You may even want to use latex gloves if you are sensitive, so they are not absorbed through your fingers.

Never go into a tanning booth or tan in the sun after using essential oils. Some oils are incredibly sensitive to sun exposure. Citrus oils especially fall into this category. Popular citrus oils to avoid the sun after using are Bergamot oil and Grapefruit oil.

As a final warning, overuse of essential oils can cause dizziness, headaches, or other side-effects. If you believe you have accidentally overdosed on any essential oil, contact emergency response services immediately. Although essential oils are mostly therapeutic, using essential oils safely is important for your safety and good health.

INHALATION METHODS

The simplest and fastest way to inhale aroma molecules of essential oil is to sniff from an open vial, or wear it mixed with a carrier as a perfume.

A more intense delivery to the brain is achieved by placing a few drops of oil in the palm, cupping hands over the nose and inhaling and breathing in and out deeply through the nose, keeping the mouth closed.

Diffusing oil into the air is the most thorough method of inhalation. A wide variety of diffusers ranges from a pottery bowl heated by a candle underneath to an electrically heated bowl. There also is a nebulizer, vaporizer, humidifier, wick inhaler, plug-in atomizer with wick refills, room spray, potpourri, pillow or linen sachet, and the newest trend, a multi-reed diffuser. With every diffusion method, only a few drops of oil, combined with stream or water, are all that is needed to reap therapeutic benefits.

TOPICAL APPLICATION

A full body massage, with properly diluted essential oil, is the most popular way to apply essential oil to the skin. Targeted relief can be achieved by applying essential oils to reflexology points on soles of the feet and palms. With a headache, oils can be massaged into the temples. For abdominal relief, a localized massage relaxes muscles used in digestion and elimination.

A leisurely soak in bath water treated with essential oil or scented bath salts is the perfect ending to a massage. Diluted essential oil can be added to a hot tub or Jacuzzi, or splashed on sauna rocks.

Essential oils added to shampoo, conditioner, soap, face cleanser, lotions and moisturizers are a wise addition to face and hair beauty regimens.

Some people like to add diluted oils to a roller bottle to apply to the skin.

DILUTING

Three to five drops of oil, added one by one, to one teaspoon of carrier oil or lotion is a good ratio. Another common dilution guide is 12 drops per ounce of carrier oil. Use less in skincare products for the face. For tub water, first dissolve the essential oil in honey, vegetable oil, half-&-half, powdered, or liquid milk. This will spread oil throughout tub and prevent it collecting in one spot.

BLENDING

When creating a blend, the main thing to remember is the nose knows. Based on your research, choose three oils that will provide the benefits you want. Experiment with them on swabs to discover a unique recipe and the quantities you want to use in a particular blend. Using only a few ingredients, mistakes can be corrected easily. With experience, add or subtract additional oils one at a time, for a maximum of five.

HOW ESSENTIAL OILS ARE MADE

Essential oils are extracted from certain plants, trees, and fruits using a technique called distillation. Since plants contain such a small amount of extract, several pounds of plants are required to provide a small bottle to consumers. The essential oils are then refined and distilled and packaged in containers that help preserve the scent and fragrance for a good amount of time. The following is a list of treatments and extract procedures that produce the essential oils for our use in aromatherapy or creams.

STEAM DISTILLATION

Steam distillation is the most popular and the oldest distillation process available. Old time, traditional aromatherapy professionals believe this method is the best way to produce the most quality extracts. This system takes dried or fresh plants and places them into a steam chamber. The steam is pressurized and then circulated in and out of the plant material. The heat from the pressurized steam causes the plant's cellular structure to open and the oils pour into a holding container. This is a delicate method since the heat must be balanced to open the plant but not too hot to destroy the delicate oil.

After the steam and oil are distilled into a container, the steam returns to a liquid while the oil creates a film at the top of the solution. Both the liquid and the oil are both therapeutic by-products of the process. The oils can be packaged as a pure essential oil extract. The water still contains oil properties, so it is used by cosmetic companies in toners and skin creams.

COLD PRESSING

Extracts from fruits like Bergamot, Grapefruit, Lemon or Limes use different forms of processing. The essential oils are mainly in the fruit's peel. The peel is rolled over a large array of sharp objects that cause the peel to burst and seep the oils. Then the fruit is squeezed and the juice contained. Like steam distillation, the essential oils rise to the top of the juice as a film. They are separated by centrifugations into containers packaged to consumers.

EFFLEURAGE

This method of extraction is used for flowers or plants that are delicate. Some plants are too delicate to withstand the heat from steam distillation. Enfleurage uses animal fat to absorb oils from the delicate flowers. As the petals are drained, more are placed on the animal fats. After the fat is saturated, the fat is treated with alcohol which solvates the essential oils. Once the mixture is contained, the alcohol will evaporate leaving behind the essential oil product.

SOLVENT EXTRACTION

Solvent extraction is the most efficient and affordable way to separate the extract from the plant. In this method, a solvent is used to saturate the plant and absorb the oils. After saturation, it is then treated with alcohol. Like enfleurage, the alcohol eventually evaporates and it leaves only the essential oils for packaging. This method is especially useful for more expensive extracts where each plant needs to be squeezed for its extract as much as possible. Although this method is the most cost-efficient, it can leave solvent in the product which can cause side-effects.

HOW TO MAKE YOUR OWN ESSENTIAL OILS

Packaged essential oils are highly potent and concentrated. Below are basic instructions on how to extract, distil, and cultivate your own essential oils.

BUY A DISTILLER

The first important item you will need is to buy is a distiller. To guess is cheap, to guess wrong is expensive. Distillers cost a few hundred dollars, so make sure the one you choose is durable and will do the job. Distillers have several components to consider. The heater is important to properly steam and heat the plants to extract the oils. The holding tank will decide how much water you will be able to use. Smaller holding tanks will mean less steam. The condenser collects the steamed mixture and holds it for cooling. Finally, the separator is used to separate the water from the oil.

Decide what plant you would like to use, and either buy it or grow it. Some expensive essential oils are only available from other countries. Before bringing non-indigenous plants into your region, research any postal or travel guidelines. Some plants are forbidden imports, due to mold, fungus, or insects that might travel with the plants.

When you receive the plant, dry the plant for the distiller. Drying the plant will dry some of the oil, but it will yield a higher extract product. Drying is a slow process and it should never be done by sunlight. Sunlight can damage the oils and render the plant useless. The distilling process should be done immediately after drying is complete.

Add the water to your distiller, and pack the plant material in the container. Don't cut or break the plants. The distiller will extract from whole plant material. Pack thick to receive enough extract.

Boil the water so steam starts to form. Keep an eye on the distiller to make sure it does not overflow. It is also important to make sure the water does not evaporate. The heat without the water can break your distiller.

You can filter the solutions by pouring the solution through a cloth fabric. This is done to remove small defects and contaminants that can cause allergies. It will also remove dirt from the solution, making it purer.

Store the oil in a container. The container for essential oils should be dark glass or stainless steel. Never use clear glass or your product can spoil more quickly. Never use plastic storage containers. The oils will damage the plastic. The essential oils should be kept in a cool, dark place away from contaminates. Most essential oils have an estimated shelf life of two years.

After the oil is removed, the remaining part of the distillation process is the hydrosol. It contains some of the oil and fragrance ingredients that offer therapeutic results. Use the water for bathwater or a light scent. Some prefer to throw the hydrosol away.

EXTRACTION

Extraction is the process used to remove oil molecules from plant material. Extraction determines an essential oil's properties, its benefits, how it's purchased and used. The four primary methods of extracting essential oils are steam or water distillation, solvent extraction, and expression.

Distillation by steam under pressure is the most efficient means of extraction. Plant material is heated, vapor forms, and when it cools the resulting liquid is essential oil. In water distillation, the plant material is covered in water and heated in a sealed container. This method takes longer than steam pressure and risks damaging delicate ingredients from longer exposure to heat. Steam distillation is the preferred and most common method of extraction.

Solvent extraction is used for delicate petals like Jasmine and Rose with a low yield of essential oil. This extraction is the end process of a method called efleurage, where petals are placed on glass and covered with an odorless fat or oil. An alternate method is to stir flowers into heated oil. Flowers are added to the mix until the oil or fat becomes saturated with flower essence, forming a substance called concrete or pomade. The pomade is soaked in alcohol which absorbs the fragrance from fat, and the two are separated. The alcohol is allowed to evaporate, leaving particulate plant matter, the absolute essence of the flower. The fat is often used in soap manufacturing. When a synthetic petrochemical like hexane or benzene is used as the solvent, the aromatherapy benefits of the absolute are inferior to those obtained with an alcohol solvent, an organic substance derived from sugar or starch.

Expression is the method for extracting oil from the rind of citrus fruit like Bergamot, Lemon, and Orange. Traditionally, this was a time-consuming project done by hand. Modern expression of rinds is mechanized. Experiment with hand expression by cutting off a segment of peel from a washed and dried piece of fruit. Pierce the peel with your fingernail, or knife tip, and over a bowl use your fingers to squeeze drops of essential oil from the rind. Store this oil in a dark glass bottle in a cool place. This is as good as any commercially bought essential oil of citrus and can be used in any form of aromatherapy.

A fifth recently discovered method of extraction uses the carbon dioxide (CO_2) process at low temperatures. This method produces highly fragrant aromas and many aromatherapists believe the process is preferable to solvent extraction. The CO_2 process requires expensive equipment making these oils costly and difficult to obtain. Opponents of this process believe the temperature in CO_2 extraction is not high enough to distil plant molecules, and that oils processed this way should be reserved for non-therapeutic uses, like soap, candles, and room deodorizers.

5% OR 10% OILS

These are a blend or formula, usually associated with more expensive essential oils. Suppliers make these costly essential oils more affordable by diluting them with a carrier oil. The percentage does not refer to the quality of an essential oil but indicates its quantity. For example, a 1-ounce bottle described as 5% Rose absolute in Jojoba will have 30 drops (1.5 ml) of pure Rose absolute and 95% Jojoba oil.

When creating your own mixtures, the recommendation is 12 drops of essential oil to 1-ounce carrier oil. With practice and test patches on your skin, you can adjust the ratio to meet your needs.

FRAGRANCE &PERFUME OILS

Fragrance oils, also called fragrant oils or perfume oils, are synthetically compounded aromas that simulate natural aromas. They should not be confused with pure essential oils. The scents might replicate natural scents, and have qualities of familiarity, richness, complexity and endurance, but are specifically formulated for addition to perfume, soap, candles, skin care, hair products, room deodorizers and household cleaners. They have no value nor application in aromatherapy. Some good examples of so-called essential oils are China Rain, Forest, Black Rose, Lily-of-the-Valley, and Vanilla. These are fragrance, or perfume, oils commonly made from synthetic chemicals.

HYDROSOLS

Hydrosol (also called hydrolat— floral or flower water) is the water or vapor by-product of distillation. It contains the fragrance of an essential oil and has the same benefits. Hydrosols are valuable skin-care products, especially when used as skin care with essential oils. Flower waters for cosmetic purposes are made, for example, from Chamomile, Neroli, and Rose petals.

NEAT

Most essential oils are too strong to use undiluted and this warning often appears, "Do not apply neat." The rare exceptions are Lavender and Tea Tree oil which are safe when applied directly to the skin.

ORGANIC OILS

Technically, organic essential oils must meet the same standards applied to organic food and bear the USDA green-and-white circular seal that appears on food products. This means plants must be grown without the use of chemical fertilizers or pesticides, and cannot be processed with artificial, synthetic or chemical additives or preservatives. If roses, for instance, are grown organically but their essential oil is extracted with a petrochemical or synthetic solvent, the resulting essential oil will not be organic.

The term organic is used loosely and confused with words like 100% natural, pure, chemical-free, highest- or finest-quality, no pesticides, all-herbal, grown wild, and unsprayed. These terms are not synonymous even though they are used interchangeably. The only way to verify you are getting organic essential oils is to look for the USDA seal or ask the dealer if they can certify a particular product is organically grown and manufactured.

In aromatherapy, experts disagree whether organic essential oils have a superior aroma or are more valuable than non-organic oils. Essential oils are concentrated and might hold onto high concentrations of contaminants, however, no scientific evidence supports this. When oils become water or alcohol distilled steam, molecules of pesticide and fertilizer are too large to pass through the distillation process. Theoretically, only pesticides sprayed during or after harvesting, two unlikely events, could survive distillation.

Whether to use organic essential oils is as personal as one's decision about organic food. They are more expensive than non-organic, sometimes more than double the cost.

ESSENTIAL OILS BUYING GUIDE

CHOOSING ESSENTIAL OILS

There are more than 3,000 essential oils, but only around 300 are used in aromatherapy. Of those, there are 101 major essential oils traded on the global market.

The average arsenal of essential oils contains approximately one or two dozen individual oils and five to seven blends.

A good number for the beginner or novice is ten. But which ten? Every manufacturer, merchant, author and practitioner have a Top 10 list of essential oils, and no two lists are the same.

Essential oils are listed myriad ways— alphabetically, botanically, aromatically, chemically, according to the ailment, and physical body systems.

Health, well-being, and beauty are about balance, and ill-health and discomfort are about imbalance or opposing forces. In the most primary sense, energy is both positive and negative and these two forces balance each other. Heat balances cold, dark balances light and opposites attract. One way to categorize essential oils is how they bring balance and return equilibrium.

Physical, mental, and emotional problems, viewed as either positive or negative states, need an antidote. Treating illnesses collectively as a duality, essential oils can be sorted as either negative (relaxing, calming, tension-relieving, or sedating) or positive (stimulating, rejuvenating, invigorating, or awakening).

When you decide to use essential oils to help your mood, stress, or physical illness, it is hard to know which one is right for you. Essential oils come in many versions, and outcomes will be unique between individuals. Some help your mental fatigue, others relieve stress, and others are used as topical creams to alleviate scars or acne.

The first thing to consider when choosing an essential oil is to inhale the fragrance. Some scents are pungent, others are citrus, and others have a flowery smell. If any of these scents bother you, then the essential oil will not promote relaxation. Be familiar with the fragrance before you buy. When testing the scent, make sure to keep it a few inches away if full strength. Undiluted essential oils can give you a headache.

When testing scents, take frequent breaks. Do not continually inhale too many fragrances or they may cause dizziness or headaches. You also may not be able to distinguish between the scents after overstimulating your senses.

Avoid buying essential oils that are priced by the size of the bottle. Some grocery stores and pharmacies have a collection of essential oils priced the same. Some essential oils are rare and expensive. If a company sells all its essential oils at the same price, the chances the more expensive oils are not genuine is increased. They may also have been distilled with cheaper methods that leave some of the by-products in the packaging.

If you are sensitive to oily solvents, then avoid using essential oils diluted with vegetable oil. Although this is a recommended way to dilute the extracts, it leaves an oily residue behind. To test if an essential oil has been diluted this way, place a tiny drop on a piece of paper. If it leaves behind a residue as the drop slides off the paper, then it has likely been diluted with vegetable oil.

When shopping for bottles, use manufacturers that list the Latin name on the bottle. This leaves no confusion on the actual extract that is contained in the bottle. Some extracts are closely related to the common names that we know, so they are falsely advertised as the real thing. Also take note of the country. Some essential oils come from exotic places like Africa while others are native to France. This will give you an idea if it is authentic.

The best essential oils are pure. Some companies sell synthetic essential oils which can be dangerous. The synthetic oils do not have the therapeutic impact of pure essential oils. Also, the synthetic oils can cause allergies or painful headaches.

Choose pure essential oils over synthetic essential oils. Aromatherapists prefer pure oils, saying that synthetic oils do not have the same therapeutic properties. Synthetic oils are thought to cause more headaches and allergic reactions.

Containers used to store essential oils should be dark or navy blue. Clear bottles allow sunlight to enter the oils and they can spoil the extracts more quickly. Make sure to keep extracts out of sunlight and in a dry, cool place.

GETTING INFO AND PRODUCTS ONLINE

In a Google search box, type "essential oils" and "oil name" to research any oil. Be aware more expensive oils are not necessarily better. Be wary of oils sold within a multi-marketing framework.

Buyer beware. On the low end of pricing, make sure the oil is not diluted. You want the oil to be 100% pure oil and 'therapeutic,' 'aromatherapy,' 'food,' or 'medicinal' grade. Note that none of these labels are standards in the industry. If you want to be sure of the oil content, look for GC/MS information and certification on the manufacturer's website.

Look for sales, and oils packaged in groups for the best deal.

Pay attention to the size of the bottles. Oils typically come in 5ml, 10ml, and 15ml size bottles. Larger bottles start at 4 ounces. A little goes a long way, and if you are experimenting, go for the 5ml if it is less expensive. When comparing prices between manufacturers, make sure you are comparing the same size bottle.

Also, if you are used to American fluid measurements, it may be hard to guess the sizes.

Here is a helpful guide:

> 5ml is .16 an ounce
>
> 10ml is approximately a third of an ounce
>
> 15ml is approximately a half an ounce
>
> 30ml is approximately one ounce

Remember the standard rule is 12 drops per ounce. Some can be a higher concentration, but do research before your skin test to avoid burns.

WHY DO SOME OILS HAVE DIFFERENT NAMES AND HOW DOES THAT RELATE TO QUALITY?

I'm only going to talk about the three in this guide, Sandalwood Agmark, Chamomile Maroc, and Lavender French. Once you understand the general concepts of name identification, you can dive into the specifics on the internet if necessary.

Sandalwood refers to the White Sandalwood evergreen tree which grows to 50 feet in the Eastern India region. Sandalwood is a parasitic tree and obtains nutrients from several other plant species, leading to distinct differences between oils and specific naming conventions. It is known as White Sandalwood, Mysore Sandalwood, East Indian Sandalwood, Sandal, Chandan (Hindi), and Tan Xiang (Mandarin).

The environmental conditions needed by this tree are strict and mysterious. It grows in dry and rocky environments and reproduces by suckers and seeds. The trees are difficult to reproduce and must grow for at least thirty years to become suitable for harvesting. Due to a combination of the environmental requirements and the necessity of living off a host plant, Sandalwood is not easy to propagate.

Sandalwood oil is in high demand and the resource is dwindling. Sandalwood oil is one of the most-often adulterated essential oils. Due to product scarcity, its cost is rising dramatically. Trees are illegally cut, leading to trees cut too young or roots left to rot (the most valuable part of the tree to extract the oil).

When an oil is labeled Sandalwood Agmark, the Agmark means it is true Indian Sandalwood. It carries the Indian Governments' Agmark Seal which guarantees product quality, purity, and sustainable harvesting. Agmark oil is also the most expensive. You don't have to buy the purest form to get results.

With Lavender and Chamomile, the extra qualifier lets you know where the herbs were grown.

What is the difference between Bulgarian, German,

Roman, and French Lavender? The farming region, and the scent. The qualities and uses for each are similar, however, French Lavender produces more 'linalool', a chemical feature that gives French Lavender its sweet aroma and its therapeutic ability to treat insomnia by reducing stress and anxiety, and improving sleep.

Linalool has been shown to have strong anti-cancer properties. In one study, linalool was shown to have potent anti-tumor results on a commonly studied liver cancer cell line.

Moroccan Chamomile (or Chamomile Maroc) is recognized for its anti-inflammatory properties and are used to relieve symptoms of allergies, dermatitis, eczema, inflamed joints, muscles, neuralgia, skin rashes and sprains.

Roman Chamomile is mainly grown in England, but continental Europe and the United States also distil the oil.

German Chamomile is what is used to make Chamomile tea and is an excellent natural antihistamine for hay fever, asthma, and hives. If German Chamomile is brown, it was overheated during distillation and has lost the chamazulene-rich blue color, reducing its healing and anti-inflammatory properties.

Mama'd put brewed tea bags on our teeth to draw out a toothache. —Gramma Jenkins

For ear aches, blow cigar smoke into the ears. —Sweet Dottie

AROMATHERAPY & OILS DECODED

Aromatherapy is not intended as a substitute for traditional medical treatment. It's an extension of a long-established practice of treating medical conditions with plants found in nature. Aspirin evolved from experiments with the by-product of the spirea plant at the Bayer & Co. dye factory.

An enterprising chemist, Felix Hoffman, synthesized the first acetylsalicylic acid, known from earlier research to treat rheumatism successfully. We've cured cold symptoms for generations with Vicks Vaporub, whose main ingredients are synthetic forms of Mint (menthol), Laurel Tree (camphor), and Eucalyptus (eucalyptol), Cedar Leaf, Nutmeg and pine oils.

Coca-Cola was originally marketed as a nerve tonic, containing various essential oils of citrus and spices.

Aromatherapy, like all healing, is both a science and an art, providing a fascinating but sometimes overwhelming study. Basically, essential oils are aromatic molecules removed from plant material—

petals, leaves, twigs, seeds, needles, wood, resin and rind. Knowing the basic jargon of aromatherapy is the first step in understanding the remarkable way essential oils are used to treat whatever ails you, physically, cosmetically, mentally, emotionally or spiritually. Following are basic terms and concepts to help wade through a plethora of botanical and pharmacological data, which at times might seem confusing and contradictory. They are listed in alphabetical order for easy reference.

ABSOLUTE OILS

Absolutes are the alcohol-soluble, or semi-liquid oil that results from the solvent extraction process used with plants that have an unusually low yield. For instance, 1,000 pounds of flowers yield one teaspoon of Jasmine absolute. One teaspoon of Rose absolute requires 5,000 pounds of petals. Steam distillation to get an equal amount of Rose essential oil, called Rose otto (attar) requires twice that amount or 10,000 pounds of petals. Consequently, Rose otto is twice the price of Rose absolute.

BLENDED OILS

Blends, sometimes called formulas or synergies, are a manufacturer's recipe for a combination of oils targeted to treat a specific condition. There are as many pre-blended oils as there are ailments, diseases, bodily functions, moods, states of being, and levels of spiritual growth. The selection is unlimited. Professional aromatherapists have their own recipes, based on knowledge and experience. Experts advise the novice in aromatherapy to study the profiles of individual essential oils and invent their own treatments based on research and personal preference.

The blends are excellent if you want to experiment with premixed formulas, but it will be as time-consuming as learning about individual oils. No two blended formulas will be the same. When you compare blended remedies, you might find common ingredients, but their proportions will not be the same.

CARRIER OILS

Whether essential oils are thick and oily or thin and watery, they share a common chemical characteristic, they don't mix with water. Essential oils, even if they are clear and runny, will only blend with fatty oils or alcohol.

The primary way to dilute essential oils is in a carrier oil, sometimes called base oil. Carrier oils are usually pressed from seeds, nuts, vegetables or trees. Common carrier oils are Almond, Coconut, Jojoba, and Sunflower.

In most essential oil blends, the major ingredient is a carrier oil with a few drops of essential oils, which for the most part are too strong to be applied to the skin undiluted, or too expensive to use alone. A few essential oils, like Lavender or Tea Tree, are gentle enough to use as carrier oils.

Carrier oils are a way to deliver small amounts of essential oil over the entire body during the massage process. Additionally, carrier oils retain moisture and keep essential oils from evaporating too quickly when exposed to air. Diluted essential oils last longer. During massage, this means essential oils will linger and absorb slowly into the skin.

CARRIER OILS IN KENTUCKY CRONE SERUMS

POMEGRANATE SEED

Pomegranates are associated with anti-aging, and the most powerful form of pomegranate for anti-aging is its oil, and it can protect your skin from sun damage. The oil contains high concentrations of antioxidants to prevent free radical damage and slow the aging process.

Considered a potent natural treatment for skin cancer, it also helps to nourish skin, strengthen elasticity, and promote cell regeneration. It also protects and heals dry, irritated, burned, or damaged skin affected by eczema or psoriasis.

PRIMROSE

Evening Primrose oil contains the pain-relieving compound phenylalanine and is studied all over the world as a treatment for aging problems, acne, and many other diseases. It is recommended for preserving youth and preventing disease.

The gamma-linoleic acid, linoleic acid and other

nutrients in this oil are essential for cell structure. They improve the elasticity of the skin, ease the joint pain and swelling of rheumatoid arthritis, prevent neuropathy (diabetes-associated nerve damage), reduce the symptoms of eczema, helps treat acne and rosacea, and nourishes nails, scalp, and hair.

APRICOT KERNEL OIL

Apricot Kernel oil is one of the best carrier oils for skin-healing oil blends. Rich in omega-6 gamma-linolenic acid, Apricot Kernel oil helps to hydrate and nourish skin while vitamins A and E encourage regeneration of skin cells and collagen production to reduce fine lines and wrinkles. This oil is especially helpful for hydrating and healing dry skin.

SWEET ALMOND

Sweet Almond oil contains large amounts of vitamins E and K. This oil not only helps skin regenerate and preserve elasticity, it also promotes better circulation. Sweet Almond oil is odorless, light and absorbs quickly.

JOJOBA OIL

Jojoba oil contains many worthwhile ingredients, including vitamin E, vitamin B complex, silicon, chromium, copper, and zinc. Jojoba oil doesn't clog pores and is rich in iodine which fights harmful bacteria. Antioxidants soothe fine lines, wrinkles and naturally slow down other signs of aging. Jojoba oil speeds up wound closures and stimulates collagen.

Our sebaceous glands are microscopic glands in our skin that secrete an oily or waxy matter called sebum. The texture and use of sebum are similar to Jojoba oil, so as we age our sebaceous glands produce less sebum, leading to dry skin and hair, and even dandruff or itchy scalp. The oil plays the role of sebum and moisturizes our skin but also removes sticky buildup or excess oil, keeping your oil levels balanced. As an emollient, it moisturizes our skin and prevents irritations and scaly or rough patches.

ROSEHIP SEED

This oil is well-known for its high concentration of vitamin A, a retinoic acid which can help reduce wrinkles, fade fine lines, lighten age spots, and promote overall healing of damaged skin by boosting the growth rate of new cells and increasing collagen production. Please note that this is not the same as Retinol.

Rose Hip Seed oil is rich in skin-nourishing essential fatty acids including omega-6, linoleic acid, and omega-3. Linolenic acid helps improve the elasticity, texture, and appearance of skin.

Tincture of Violet works for thrush, but it will turn the kid's mouth purple. —Mama Dot

To prevent baggy arms, don't sleep with your arms over your head. —Nanny Nanda

To remove warts, cut a potato in half, rub the wart with one-half and bury the other half. Works every time. —Granma Emily

OIL PROPERTIES TERMINOLOGY

The following list only relates to conditions of the skin as all the Kentucky Crone products are for external use only. No medical claims are made by this list of essential oil properties. Please consult your doctor with any worries.

ANALGESIC—reduces pain.

ANTI-BACTERIAL—inhibits the growth of bacteria.

ANTI-BIOTIC—inhibit the growth of germs, virus, and fungi. They also effectively prohibit infections of the skin.

ANTI-CARCINOGENIC—reduces reactions in the body that cause cancer.

ANTI-ARTHRITIC—reduces swelling and pain from arthritis.

ANTI-FUNGAL—used to fight fungal infections, suppresses fungal growth.

ANTI-INFLAMMATORY—reduces inflammation of tissues due to fever or viral infection.

ANTI-MICROBIAL—inhibit microbe or viral activity,

preventing ailments resulting from microbial infection, like mumps, measles, and wound infections.

ANTI-OXIDANT—inhibits oxidation or inhibits reactions promoted by oxygen or peroxides in the body.

ANTI-SEPTIC—promotes fast healing of wounds, cracks on the skin and heels, ulcers, eczema, and itching, and protects wounds from sepsis or tetanus.

ANTI-SPASMODIC—relaxes nerves and muscles. Quick relief for cramps, convulsions, and painful muscle contractions.

ASTRINGENT—tightens loose muscles. Can cause blood vessels to contract. Firms skin and muscles. When the blood vessels contract the flow of blood, it can reduce blood loss when wounded.

ANTI-BACTERIAL—kills bacteria and keeps your body free from microbial infections and toxins.

ANTI-RHEUMATIC—reduces swelling and other symptoms of arthritis.

ANTI-VIRAL—inhibit microbe or viral activity, preventing ailments resulting from viral infections.

CICATRISANT—reduces scars and other marks on the skin.

CIRCULATORY—stimulates blood circulation to supply oxygen to parts of the body.

CORDIAL—invokes warmth.

CYTOPHYLACTIC—promotes the generation of new cells and stimulates health.

DEODORANT—reduces or covers odors.

DEPURATIVE—cleans the blood of toxins and acts as a detoxifier or blood purifier to remove common toxins like uric acid, heavy metals, pollutants and certain compounds and hormones produced by the body.

DIAPHORETIC—it increases perspiration and keeps your body free from toxins, extra salt and excess water from your body. Sweating also cleans the skin pores and helps harmful gasses like nitrogen escape.

DISINFECTANT—inhibit the growth of germs, virus, and fungi. They also effectively prohibit infections, including those of the skin.

DIURETIC—increases both the frequency and volume of urination. Useful for those suffering from an accumulation of water in the body, or swelling due to minor or chronic renal failure. Reduces blood pressure and removes extra salts and dangerous toxins like uric acid from the body.

FEBRIFUGE—lowers body temperature to prevent or reduce fever.

HYPOTENSIVE—reduces blood pressure.

IMMUNE BOOSTER—strengthens and activates the immune system and protects from infections.

NERVINE—quiets nervous excitement.

RELAXANT—relieves muscular or nervous tension.

RUBEFACIENT—increases blood circulation and reddens skin, causing irritation on the skin if applied in excess.

SEDATIVE—sedates and soothes. It is good for calming inflammation, trauma, and shock. It also promotes sleep and relaxes the body.

STIMULANT—stimulates the body, helps overcome fatigue, dizziness, and depression. Increases the activity of the brain and neurons, nervous system, and secretions from the endocrine and exocrine glands.

SUDORIFIC—produces heavy sweating or perspiration for removal of toxins, excess salt, and water. This cleans the skin pores and openings of sweat and sebum glands, aiding in preventing acne and other skin diseases.

TONIC—helps the systems function properly, boosts immunity, and strengthens. It tones everything, including the muscles, tissues, and skin.

VASOCONSTRICTOR—narrows blood vessels and can maintain or increase blood pressure.

VULNERARY—helps wounds heal faster and protects from infections.

INFO ON RELAXANTS

BERGAMOT

Bergamot, grown chiefly in Calabria, Italy, is a sour tasting citrus fruit whose rind ironically produces a sweet, lemony oil with a gentle, refreshing fragrance. Bergamot has been cultivated in South America and the United States, but the quality is incomparable to fruit grown in southern Italy's unique soil. The green or yellow oil is an ingredient in many colognes and perfumes and is used in the production of Earl Grey tea, giving the drink its characteristic aroma. Bergamot is considered the finest citrus oil and is sometimes called the sunny oil. It has a soothing, calming effect and simultaneously energizes and uplifts the spirit.

Bergamot is good for skin conditions like eczema, psoriasis, herpes, acne and oily skin. It's excellent for cystitis and urinary tract infections, and for reducing fever. It balances the appetite, and is useful for weight reduction and stimulating the appetite.

The anti-depressant qualities of Bergamot make it ideal for Seasonal Affective Disorder (SAD) on cold, gray days. Its mild, sedating effect helps control anger, relieve stress, reduce nervous tension, fear, and anxiety.

Do not use Bergamot on the skin undiluted. Use it with a carrier oil, lotion or bathwater. A few drops of oil in a solution is enough.

Since most Bergamot oil is photosensitive, to prevent severe skin reaction, do not use on the skin within twelve hours of sun exposure. Oil labeled Bergapten Free or Bergamot FCF (Furo-Coumarin Free) is safe even in direct sunlight and will not cause a reaction.

CHAMOMILE

Chamomile oil, a deep-blue substance extracted from white, daisy-like flowers, is a sweet, herbal aroma with a fruity, bitter undertone. When dried, the flowers are used to make Chamomile tea, a drink used to promote relaxation. There are many varieties of Chamomile, but the German and French plants are believed to have the best medicinal value. Chamomile is soothing, calming and balancing with a gentle rejuvenating or restorative effect.

This is one of the few safe essential oils for use with infants and children, and during pregnancy.

Chamomile oil is an anti-inflammatory agent useful in treating skin rash, blisters, and allergies, including eczema. It also has analgesic properties and is useful in the treatment of deep, persistent pain, muscle tension, or spasm. It is excellent for reducing stomachache, pre-menstrual cramping, and headache, including a migraine. Because of its gentleness, a few drops diluted in boiling water can make a soothing eye compress to treat conjunctivitis or tired eyes.

Chamomile's calming and sedating effect make it a traditional ingredient in massage oil to promote overall relaxation. It's a favorite for balancing mood swings, emotionality, anxiety, nervous tension, and insomnia.

Chamomile oil that is no longer blue and has begun turning green is not fresh and should be discarded.

CLARY SAGE

Clary Sage, commonly called salvia, is a tall herb with purple-green, hairy leaves, and a profusion of small white or pale violet flowers. Steaming the petals and leaves yields a sweet, musky oil with nutty, floral tones. It is the most euphoric of essential oils, uplifting, intoxicating, deeply relaxing, and revitalizing.

Clary Sage oil is an excellent analgesia for abdominal and stomach pain, including menstrual cramps, menopausal symptoms like hot flashes, and labor pain. Clary Sage relieves a headache, including a migraine, and is an effective chest liniment to soothe asthma. It is often used to treat dandruff and promote healthy scalp and hair.

Clary Sage oil can produce a drug-like high, and is a powerful aid in treating depression, anxiety, and melancholy. It is useful in reducing the stress that diminishes sexuality and thus is considered an aphrodisiac. This oil also aids in focusing the mind and results in more creative thinking, restful sleep, and vivid, pleasant dreams. Clary Sage is often used to achieve a meditative state.

Use of euphoric oil like Clary Sage is not compatible with alcohol consumption or recreational drug use.

- This oil should be avoided throughout pregnancy and never used on infants or children under 18.

FRANKINCENSE

The Frankincense tree grows in India and Middle Eastern and African countries, including Oman, Egypt, and Saudi Arabia. Its milky-white resin hardens into orange-brown tears, which when steamed produce an essential oil with a fresh, woody, fragrance with balsamic, smoky tones. Frankincense has been used for centuries in purification rites of Judaic, Christian, and Islamic religions to remove negativity, and was a gift of the Magi to the infant Jesus. This oil, used as a disinfectant and perfume fixative, is also an ingredient for incense. Generally, it is calming, uplifting, and rejuvenating.

Frankincense is one of the best essential oils for skin care, and an excellent therapy for dry, sensitive or mature skin that has lost its elasticity.

This oil is used to restore skin tone and prevent wrinkles. It also helps reduce scars and stretch marks. Additionally, Frankincense oil is used to treat asthma, bronchitis, coughing spell, sinusitis, cold and sore throat.

This is the most valuable essential oil for inducing slow, deep breathing, lessening fear, and developing courage and emotional strength. It is also an aid for eliminating sadness, anxiety, nervous tension, stress, and nightmares. Frankincense inspires prayer, meditation and mystical states of mind.

LAVENDER

Lavender oil comes from the purple or violet flowers of a bushy shrub with gray or green leaves. The colorless to pale yellow-green oil has a clean, floral fragrance, slightly sweet, with subtle balsamic or woody undertones. Known as the Queen of Essential Oils, or the cure-all oil, Lavender is the best all-around essential oil. It blends well with other essences and boosts their effectiveness. If you can have only one oil, make it Lavender. This oil, believed to activate the pineal gland in the brain, balances and normalizes body functions and emotions, and has been used for thousands of years for its soothing, calming, and relaxing effect. Lavender is often used in skin care products, perfume, soap and household cleaners. It can be used safely on children and infants when diluted in a carrier oil or lotion.

Lavender is an excellent analgesic for muscle ache and spasm and headache when used in massage oil or bathwater. It is effective for relieving symptoms of cold, sinus congestion and bronchitis, and for hindering virus and infection. Oil of Lavender can be applied undiluted (neat) directly on flesh wounds and burns, including sunburn, to relieve pain, combat infection, and speed healing and skin restoration. Lavender is both a treatment for insect bites and an insect repellent. Other skin conditions treated with Lavender are acne and itching due to allergies.

The aroma of Lavender helps control irritability, anger, anxiety, mood swings, hyperactivity, and insomnia. The cooling effect of this soothing oil aids insight, rationality, clear thinking, and meditation.

Lavender should be avoided during the first three months of pregnancy.

MARJORAM

Marjoram, a bushy herb with dark silver-green leaves, downy stem, and clusters of tiny, pinkish white flowers yields a colorless oil with a spicy, warm, woody aroma. It has been used in perfume, ointment, and as a food flavoring since Ancient Egypt. Marjoram is known as the great comforter for its strong and powerful sedating effect.

Marjoram helps with all types of pain because it dilates blood vessels and creates a warming effect to improve circulation. It is successful in reducing sharp, steady pain from a migraine headache, sore muscles, stiff joints, even chronic pain from arthritis and rheumatism. An abdominal massage with Marjoram oil relieves constipation and flatulence. Marjoram's heavily sedating property is anaphrodisiac and helps reduce sexual desire during celibacy.

Emotionally, Marjoram oil is effective when dealing with grief, extreme depression, or loneliness. Marjoram is suggested for hyperactivity (ADD/ADHD), hysteria, obsession (OCD), trauma (PTS), and insomnia. Inhaling this soothing aroma gives comfort, solace, fortitude, inner strength, and endurance.

Marjoram can be numbing and should be used with discretion. Excessive, or long-term use should be avoided to prevent dulling of the senses.

Marjoram should be avoided throughout pregnancy.

NEROLI

Neroli, also called Orange Blossom, is the pale yellow oil from deeply fragrant white flowers of the Seville Orange. It has a delicate, fresh floral fragrance with a strong, bittersweet undertone, and is an ingredient in many perfumes. The oil is associated with innocence and purity, like the blossom, a traditional wedding flower from which it is extracted. The fragrance emanating from the bridal bouquet is believed to soothe the nerves of an anxious bride or groom. The aroma is calming, uplifting and mildly hypnotic. This hauntingly beautiful fragrance is one of the costliest oils.

Neroli oil is a cell regenerator and is effective in rejuvenating all skin types, especially mature, dry and sensitive skin. Neroli tones facial skin and muscle, making it a choice ingredient in skin-care products, massage, or bath oil. A Neroli massage in the abdominal region will relieve intestinal spasms related to diarrhea.

Neroli is the recommended choice of aromatherapists for treating chronic anxiety, disappointment, and shock. It helps soften depression, despair, panic attacks, hysteria and post-traumatic stress (PTS), and instills confidence, initiative, and optimism. Neroli is a subtle aphrodisiac, helpful in overcoming shyness, nerves, or fear of sexual encounter.

The cheerful, uplifting oil aids meditation, creative thinking and healing on all levels of body, mind, and spirit.

ROSE

Rose bushes yield an essential oil from flower petals, using petals ranging from pale pink to deep scarlet red. The most common species for aromatherapy are the Damascus, Cabbage or French Rose. Rose otto, obtained by water distillation, is the most expensive essential oil on the market, between $500 and $1,400 an ounce, or $1.25 to $4.00 a drop. This clear to pale yellow oil has a delicate, subtle aroma that is sweet and spicy.

Rose absolute, distilled with solvent (alcohol), varies in color from orange to brown. It has a deep, dusky, and honeyed aroma, much stronger than Rose otto, but available at half the price. Some aromatherapists consider Rose absolute inferior, but other than a difference in fragrance, the properties and benefits of Rose otto and Rose absolute are the same.

The Rose is considered by many the most royal of flowers, the finest and most elegant flower in the garden. It traditionally symbolizes true love and its essential oil is a tonic for the physical heart and emotions. It is a tender, uplifting and soothing aroma that has been used for centuries to heal both heart and soul.

A Rose oil massage or bath is a preferred treatment for female reproductive problems including premenstrual cramps and emotionality (PMS), menopause, and postpartum depression. Rose oil is also a choice ingredient in skin-care products for all skin types, but especially for treating mature, dry or sensitive skin. This oil is an aphrodisiac for both men and women, soothing sexual apprehension and inspiring confidence in one's ability to express sensuality.

Essential oil of Rose softens sadness, disappointment, and grief while nurturing and strengthening the inner spirit. It creates a comforting feeling to experience and express love toward others, and the self.

Rose oil should be avoided in early pregnancy, especially if there is a history of miscarriage, but it is perfectly safe in the second and third trimesters.

SANDALWOOD

Sandalwood oil is distilled from roots and heartwood from the inner part of the Sandalwood tree, an evergreen whose wood is among the strongest and heaviest in the world. Its pale to dark yellow essential oil is the richest and longest lasting of essential oils and the beautiful fragrance is strengthened with time, rather than becoming rancid as most oils when they age. The sweet, woody aroma with touches of balsam and spice has a balancing, harmonizing effect on the psyche, and has been used in religious rituals for thousands of years to aid prayer and meditation. Sandalwood is appealing to both male and female senses and is widely used to make perfume and incense. The fragrance is erotic, relaxing, and uplifting.

Indian Sandalwood is the finest and most desirable. However, it has become an endangered species and its oil is costly. Australian Sandalwood oil, roughly half the price of Indian Sandalwood, is considered a satisfactory and comparable substitute by most aromatherapy experts.

Sandalwood is the main essential oil for treating bronchitis and laryngitis, because of its antiseptic, soothing and calming properties. It is also used for the treatment of urinary and bladder infections and fluid retention. Its astringent and balancing quality make Sandalwood suitable for treating acne and other skin and scalp conditions resulting from dry, flaky skin. Sandalwood in massage oil or bathwater is an overall body and mind soother, good for tension headaches and insomnia.

Sandalwood relieves sadness, aggression, and obsessive thinking. It's a powerful aphrodisiac, especially when frigidity or impotence result from stress, depression or feelings of isolation.

Sandalwood oil should not be applied undiluted.

SPEARMINT

Essential oil of spearmint is distilled from the pink or lilac flowers at the head of this busy herb with spear-shaped green leaves that grow to around three feet. The pale yellow-green oil has a fresh, minty aroma, similar to peppermint but sweeter and milder. This is an excellent, less harsh alternative to Peppermint for children. It's a common flavoring in chewing gum, candy, food, and medication because of its sweet, cooling, and calming effect. Spearmint tea makes an excellent bedtime drink. Ancient Greeks used Spearmint in bathwater for its antiseptic and refreshing properties.

Spearmint essential oil works well for chronic respiratory problems, like bronchitis, sinusitis, and accompanying headache or chest pain. It is also used for common digestive problems caused by tension or spasm. When massaged on the abdomen, this oil will relax stomach muscles and relieve hiccups, nausea, vomiting, flatulence, constipation, or diarrhea, and treats motion sickness. Spearmint is excellent for whitening teeth and promoting healthy gum tissue. When added to a facial cleanser, Spearmint clears and tightens pores, leaving skin toned and firm.

Oil of Spearmint's uplifting and refreshing properties make it a good choice for relieving mental fatigue and mild depression. Spearmint also brings a feeling of balance and tranquility during periods of stress or anxiety.

Although Spearmint is a common flavoring in foods and over-the-counter medications, essential oil of Spearmint, as with all essential oils, should be ingested only under the direction of a licensed health practitioner.

Spearmint might irritate eyes or sensitive skin, even when diluted in a carrier oil.

TEA TREE

Tea Tree is a shrub with needlelike leaves. The color varies from medium green to yellow. Tea Tree's bark is papery and white, so the shrub is sometimes known as Paper Bark. The essential oil extracted from Tea Tree leaves and twigs is pale yellow with a pungent, spicy, aroma, like nutmeg, and has a slight camphor odor. Oil of Tea Tree is the most medicinal essential oil for fighting all three infectious organisms: bacteria, viruses, and fungi. Its powerful antiseptic plus immunogenic properties make it a preferred choice for combating various illnesses and ailments. This is an excellent all-around first aid ointment. Tea Tree oil produces penetrating warmth and healing both physically and emotionally.

Tea Tree oil can be applied undiluted to treat skin rash, athletes foot, nail fungus, cold sores, herpes, insect bites, head lice, skin abrasions, and acne. Vaginal yeast infection (candida) can be treated with warm Tea Tree baths and regular abdominal massage with Tea Tree in a carrier oil. With steam inhalation and gargling, this oil soothes cold symptoms and sore throat. Used routinely, it prevents colds from developing into bronchitis, sinusitis or laryngitis. Regular baths and massage with Tea Tree oil help boost the immune system, especially in cases of long-term, debilitating illnesses like mononucleosis or Epstein-Barr virus. Tea Tree, mixed with Aloe Vera gel, reduces the pain and discomfort associated with shingles.

Tea Tree's powerful aroma clears the mind, aids concentration, and counters fatigue. This oil also inspires self-confidence, helps dispel the gloom of chronic illness, and fosters a positive, creative attitude toward healing. It also provides a subtle feeling of inner strength and endurance.

Tea Tree oil should be used in moderation—a maximum of 4 drops in bathwater, and 2% in massage oil or lotion.

- This oil might irritate sensitive skin.

YLANG-YLANG

The essential oil of Ylang-Ylang is extracted from large yellow tropical flowers of the Cananga tree which bloom profusely year-round in Indonesia. Translated from Malayan, Ylang-Ylang means flower of flowers. This pale yellow clear oil has an intensely sweet, almond and floral fragrance, with an exotic, woody and balsamic note. It has an exotic, seductive smell which is soothing, euphoric and sedating, making Ylang-Ylang a popular ingredient with perfumers and confectioners. Ylang-Ylang extra is the highest grade of this oil.

The primary medicinal use of Ylang-Ylang is the treatment of high blood pressure (hypertension), heart palpitations, and rapid breathing. Ylang-Ylang is an ingredient in skin and hair care products for the treatment of excessive oiliness. This oil is a powerful aphrodisiac, useful for healing impotence and frigidity when massaged on the abdomen and groin. The sweet, rich fragrance helps release inhibition and evoke passion.

Ylang-Ylang is useful to reduce general stress and tension. It also helps overcome sadness, frustration and anger, and more severe emotional problems including panic attacks and post-traumatic stress (PTS). By creating a feeling of peace and tranquility, Ylang-Ylang unlocks repressed feelings and aids in meditation, creative thinking, and artistic expression. A few drops of Ylang-Ylang in bath water before bedtime helps relax both mind and body, making it a choice treatment for insomnia.

Use Ylang-Ylang in tiny amounts and for short periods of time. Extended or excessive use might result in a headache or nausea.

Blending with a citrus oil, like Bergamot or Neroli, helps prevent negative side-effects.

Cutting the pieces into smaller ones never makes a jigsaw puzzle simpler.
—Meemaw Crone

Mutton tallow to keep your hard working hands soft. Good for diaper rash too. Tallow is the rendered lard from sheep fat. Pure lanolin.
—Granma Mary

BASIC ESSENTIAL OILS

BASIL

Basil, sometimes called Sweet Basil or Holy Basil, is an aromatic herb with yellow-green leaves and tiny white flowers, yielding a watery, pale yellow essential oil. It has a sweet, light mint aroma with hints of licorice or anise, giving it a spicy, fruity, balsamic fragrance. Oil of Basil is similar to oil of Rosemary, but gentler and subtler. It's a mild stimulant that awakens the senses and restores stamina. In India, Basil is a sacred herb grown as a house plant to protect the dwelling and the spirit of its inhabitants.

Basil is an anti-spasmodic, useful for muscle and digestive spasms when added to massage oil. This is an excellent cure for menstrual cramps, tension, and chest congestion. Basil is also used to counter physical exhaustion, especially from long-term, debilitating illness. This is a good, overall pick-me-up tonic when energy reserves are depleted.

Mental fatigue is eased by Basil oil, which aids

quick thinking and decision making. This is a gentle, all-around mental stimulant useful in countering depression and apathy, and psychic exhaustion or ennui. It's also an aid for clearing the mind before meditation.

Basil should be avoided throughout pregnancy, on hyper-sensitive skin, and children under the age of sixteen.

Use Basil sparingly—no more than 2% (6 drops to 1/2 oz.) of carrier oil or lotion. Avoid prolonged use and avoid applying undiluted.

CINNAMON LEAF

The leaves of the Cinnamon evergreen tree are used to obtain the essential oil of Cinnamon, a yellow, watery substance. Cinnamon bark is highly fragrant, and its dark red and brown essential oil is readily available, however, it's highly irritating on most skin and is seldom recommend for aromatherapy. Essential oil of Cinnamon Leaf is aromatic, with a harsh, sweet and spicy fragrance, peppery and resembling Clove, but stronger and sharper. Cinnamon is used extensively to flavor food and medicine. Cinnamon Leaf oil is exhilarating, inspiring and reviving.

Used regularly in a diffuser or vaporizer, Cinnamon oil is an excellent preventive for colds and infections from bacteria, virus or fungus. It also speeds recovery during respiratory illness. An abdominal massage with oil containing Cinnamon Leaf aids various problems caused by sluggish digestion, including flu symptoms and flatulence. Cinnamon, either in massage oil or bathwater, is helpful for anyone with poor circulation who suffer from cold hands and feet. This oil warms the body and soul with positive energy. Massaged on joints and spine, Cinnamon is a successful remedy for arthritis pain and stiffness.

Cinnamon has life-affirming properties which make it an excellent remedy for feelings of isolation, sadness, lethargy, and listlessness. It brings courage, optimism, and renewed enthusiasm for life's pleasures.

Cinnamon Leaf oil should be avoided on sensitive skin.

- Use sparingly—no more than 3 drops in bathwater or added to 1/2 oz. massage oil or lotion.

CLOVE BUD

The Clove is a small, busy evergreen with dark green, aromatic leaves, bearing fragrant red flowers and purple berries. Rose-pink buds at the center of the blossoms are sun-dried and then distilled to obtain the essential oil of Clove, a fresh, sweet, spicy fragrance similar to Cinnamon, but not as fiery or intense. This pale yellow oil has been an ingredient in perfume, medicine, and food for thousands of years dating back to ancient Egypt, China, and Rome. Clove's aroma is mysterious, intriguing, gently stimulating, and revitalizing. Clove is also analgesic, warming, and comforting.

Clove oil is a traditional home cure for toothache pain. Applied to gum tissue or an aching tooth, Clove has mild anesthetic properties. It also is an effective breath freshener and cold preventive, because of its antiseptic quality. A Clove oil massage is effective in treating muscle ache and joint stiffness associated with rheumatism and arthritis. A reliable cure for winter chills, and the blahs is a warm soak with Clove bath oil. Clove also works as an appetite stimulant and for the relief of flatulence, indigestion, and nausea.

Clove is excellent for mental and emotional negativity worsened by a physical ailment. Generally, it's an excellent tonic for energizing and reviving the psyche and restoring a positive attitude.

- Avoid using on sensitive or dry skin.
- Use sparingly—maximum three drops in bathwater, or 1/2-ounce massage oil or lotion.

EUCALYPTUS

Roughly twenty of more than 700 species of Eucalyptus are used in aromatherapy, each with subtle differences. The Eucalyptus tree is a tall evergreen, sometimes 100 feet (30 meters) high, with dark green leaves. Eucalyptus oil is colorless to pale yellow. The penetrating aroma of Eucalyptus oil is sharp, camphorated, balsamic, and woody. Lemon Eucalyptus is a different species with a distinct citrus aroma. Eucalyptus is piercing, clearing and invigorating. It is one of few essential oils whose potency increases with age rather than deteriorates.

Eucalyptus is the most popular essential oil for decongestion from colds, bronchitis, and sinusitis, whether the infection is viral, bacterial or fungal. Used with steam inhalation, Eucalyptus clears the respiratory system and relieves accompanying sore throat, headache, and neuralgia. Eucalyptus oil kills airborne bacteria and is a good room disinfectant and deodorizer when used in a vaporizer or diffuser. Essential oil of Eucalyptus is also used as an insect repellent and treatment for insect bites. Skin rashes and conditions including shingles respond well to Eucalyptus added to bathwater. It's also effective when blended with Bergamot for the treatment of herpes and cold sores.

The purifying and uplifting property of Eucalyptus oil makes it an antidote for both mental exhaustion and emotional constriction. It's also a good psychic cleanser for removing negative energy in the home. The fragrance of this oil, especially Lemon Eucalyptus, is a powerful aid to focus the mind and maintain concentration. Eucalyptus is also used to clear the mind before meditation or during prayer.

GERANIUM

The ornamental garden Geranium does not yield an essential oil, and only one of over 700 varieties of Geranium is used in aromatherapy. Essential oil is obtained from the entire Geranium plant—stalks, hairy serrated leaves, and clusters of florets ranging from pink to magenta and red. This light green oil is Lemony and herbal, with soft hints of Rose. Far less expensive than essential oil of Rose, Geranium is an economical substitute. It is often used by perfumers to extend Rose oils efficacy. The aroma is gently refreshing, uplifting, harmonizing, and equalizing. It comforts and creates a sense of security and stability.

Geranium stimulates the adrenal cortex and corrects hormonal imbalance, including menstrual cramps and menopausal symptoms. Its antiseptic quality aids in detoxifying the lymph system and healing minor flesh wounds. As a beauty aid, Geranium regulates skin glands and prevents excessive oil production. Its gentle stimulating action improves circulation and acts on the urinary system as a mild diuretic. Added to massage oil, Geranium is effective in reducing cellulite. It's also a good deodorant, room freshener, and insect repellent.

Oil of Geranium works as an antidepressant, controls mood swings, nervousness, and anxiety. It combats mental fatigue because of stress and overwork. Geranium controls the flow of energy in the body and balances the psyche emotionally, mentally, and physically.

JASMINE

Jasmine is a flowering shrub with fine green leaves and delicate white blossoms. Jasmine oil is extracted only with solvent, which produces Jasmine absolute, the only Jasmine essential oil. This dark orange oil is a powerful, exotic floral with a sweet honey undertone. It takes roughly 1,000 pounds of flowers to produce less than two ounces of Jasmine absolute, making this one of the most expensive essential oils. Jasmine is picked at night when its perfume is strongest, giving it the title Queen of the Night. Oil of Jasmine is euphoric and mildly hypnotic. Its powerful aphrodisiac quality made it Cleopatra's choice perfume for wooing Marc Anthony. Empress Josephine used Jasmine to lure Napoleon Bonaparte. Jasmine oil is intoxicating, liberating, and revitalizing.

Jasmine is an excellent skin-care ingredient, suited to mature skin. A few drops of Jasmine absolute in a warm bath eases muscle spasm, joint stiffness, and the pain of sprained ligaments. Jasmine effectively treats the reproductive systems of both men and women. An abdominal or back massage with Jasmine oil eases labor pain during childbirth and helps relieve the discomfort of an enlarged prostate gland. The powerful aphrodisiac action of Jasmine absolute can reignite passion in the most troubled sexual relationships.

Oil of Jasmine, an antidepressant of a stimulating nature, is the best choice for restoring confidence in those who suffer debilitating wavering, inactivity, and indecision. Jasmine dispels fear, paranoia, and pessimism. The positive qualities of Jasmine unlock repressed emotions, elevate thinking, and foster insight and wisdom.

LEMON

Lemon essential oil is cold-pressed from the rind of the common citrus fruit which grows on small trees year-round. This pale yellow-green oil should not be confused with oil of Lemongrass, Lemon-petit grain, or Lemon Balm, which have different properties and uses in aromatherapy. Oil of Lemon's fragrance is a light, clean, slightly sweet scent similar to fresh lemon rind but richer, more intense and longer lasting. This oil is used extensively in perfume, medicine, personal care products, household cleaners, and as a food flavoring. Lemon is often blended with other flavorings and fragrances to enhance their properties. The aroma is invigorating, refreshing, and purifying.

Lemon oil's astringent and antibacterial qualities make it useful for cleansing wounds and detoxifying the circulatory, respiratory, and lymphatic systems. Lemon oil neutralizes acid and is useful in treating rheumatism, gout, or an overly acidic stomach. It's also useful for halting the spread of bacterial infections, colds, and sore throats.

As an ingredient in beauty products, Lemon oil is excellent for dull, oily skin, dark spots, and varicose veins. A drop or two of Lemon oil added to shampoo or final rinse water gives hair a bright, sparkling sheen, regardless of natural color. A Lemon oil bath is recommended for physical exhaustion and mental fatigue.

Lemon oil helps remove confusion and aids quick thinking, decision making, and concentration. It is excellent for clearing the mind before meditation. The aroma of Lemon clears negative vibrations and creates warm, comfortable feelings toward others.

Essential Lemon oil is photosensitive and should not be used on skin 24 hours before exposure to sunlight.

- Avoid using on sensitive skin.
- Use sparingly—maximum three drops in bathwater, 1/2 ounce of lotion, or carrier oil.

PATCHOULI

The Patchouli bush has large, soft, hairy leaves and pale pink flowers. The leaves are dried and fermented for several days before they are distilled to obtain an exotic, dark orange essential oil. The heavy fragrance is sweet, spicy and woody, slightly balsamic and smoky. Patchouli is a powerful ingredient in perfume and is used as a deodorizer and moth repellent in carpeting, clothing, and other woven fabrics. It's also an aphrodisiac for both male and female. The distinct, strong aroma is uplifting, balancing, regenerative and sensual.

Patchouli is a valuable skin care ingredient for mature, oily skin, and conditions like dandruff, dermatitis, or athletes foot. Its regenerative properties are effective in skin cell renewal, particularly with scar tissue. Patchouli treats insect and snakebites and is an effective bug repellent.

Sexual desire and passion are stimulated when Patchouli is worn as perfume, or added to oil for an abdominal massage. Patchouli helps both male impotence and female frigidity.

Patchouli is excellent for stress-related emotional imbalance, including anxiety, nervousness, and anger. It is useful for treating procrastination because of confusion, or depressive negative thoughts. Patchouli's earthy smell grounds and centers the psyche. It's used to correct spaced-out thinking and excessive daydreaming. Patchouli has been used to reduce cravings during withdrawal from drug or tobacco addiction.

PEPPERMINT

Peppermint essential oil is distilled from the pale purple flowering tops or downy leaves of the Peppermint plant. The pale green oil has a fresh penetrating smell and a hint of grass and camphor, similar to spearmint but more pungent. Peppermint is one of the oldest natural drugs, dating back thousands of years to ancient Egypt and Greece. It's used throughout the world in over-the-counter medications and to flavor food, gum, and candy. A menthol content from 50-85% gives peppermint oil its minty aroma and creates a unique sensation which simultaneously cools and stimulates. The bold action of peppermint is soothing, refreshing and energizing.

Peppermint is the principal essential oil for various digestive maladies. A gentle abdominal massage with Peppermint oil will help relieve irritable bowel syndrome, diarrhea, flatulence, constipation, colon spasm, motion sickness, vomiting or nausea. Peppermint's analgesic properties have relieved headaches for many years. Diluted in a carrier oil, Peppermint oil rubbed on temples, forehead, and neck even helps a chronic migraine headache. A Peppermint massage is also good for arthritis, muscle aches or spasms in legs or feet, and menstrual cramps. As a decongestant and expectorant, Peppermint oil massaged on the chest will treat colds, cough, bronchitis, sinusitis and asthma. The anti-viral property of peppermint fights influenza, herpes, yeast infection, and athletes foot. As a powerful antiseptic, peppermint oil treats bad breath, tooth decay, and gum disease.

Peppermint oil when inhaled improves mental clarity, alertness, concentration, and intuitive thinking. It is excellent for treating mental fatigue, feelings of insecurity, inferiority, and apathy. It is an excellent restorative tonic and an overall pick-me-up.

Essential oil of Peppermint might cause an allergic reaction, especially on sensitive skin, and should only be used in a carrier oil, lotion or bathwater.

- Avoid using oils or lotions with Peppermint oil on children under five years old. A severe choking reaction to menthol might occur.

PINE NEEDLE

The towering Scotch pine, an evergreen with characteristic red bark, yields oil from its branches, cones, and needle-like leaves. The preferred source of essential oil for aromatherapy is pine needles. This colorless clear oil has a fresh, earthy, balsamic fragrance with a subtle touch of turpentine. Pine oil is a powerful antiseptic traditionally added to soap, cleaners, deodorants, and men's cologne. It is used in saunas and steam baths for a dual cleansing/energizing effect. The piercing aroma is revitalizing, warming, and invigorating.

Pine is a primary essential oil for clearing phlegm from the lungs and respiratory system and is used for simple colds, and chronic sinusitis, bronchitis, hay fever, and allergy. Pine is antiseptic and kills both bacteria and viruses. Added to a vaporizer, Pine will ease breathing for asthma sufferers and disinfect air in a room. Pine also provides a stimulating analgesic massage for a headache or neuralgia. Pine, in a compress or massage lotion, soothes sports injuries, sprains, and muscle strain from over- exertion. A Pine bath treats cystitis and gently stimulates and revives weak kidney or bladder function, serving as a mild diuretic. It's an excellent ingredient to include in massage treatments for cellulite.

Oil of Pine is good for relieving fatigue and mental exhaustion stemming from irritability and tension. Pine oil diffused into the air clears the psyche, removing feelings of guilt, and inspiring self-confidence, acceptance, and forgiveness. A mist of Pine will clear a physical space of stagnant, negative vibrations, and provide a comfortable atmosphere for meditation.

Pine can be irritating to sensitive skin even when diluted.

ROSEMARY

Rosemary is a bushy shrub with silver-green leaves and a profusion of sky-blue flowers. This thin, colorless oil has a sweet, herbaceous aroma with touches of balsam and camphor, giving Rosemary a slightly medicinal, fresh odor. Historically, Rosemary is believed to create a shield of protection around the psyche to ward off negativity and is used in wedding and funeral rituals. Commercially, Rosemary is a traditional ingredient in hair and skin care products. Rosemary is calming, comforting, invigorating, and balancing.

A few drops of Rosemary oil in shampoo, conditioner, or rinse water will stimulate the scalp, correct dandruff, and encourage the growth of strong, healthy hair with natural shine and highlights. Rosemary in facial products will revitalize mature, dull skin. A warming Rosemary body massage stimulates circulation, loosens stiff joints, alleviates muscle aches and spasms, and reduces the pain of neuralgia, arthritis, rheumatism, and gout. This oil has powerful antiseptic qualities when diffused into the air, and halts the spread of airborne infection. A morning bath with Rosemary oil helps jump-start the day, even relieving an alcohol hangover.

Rosemary is the strongest essential oil for aiding brain function. Rosemary provides mental structure, stability, and strength during times of emotional stress, negativity, and confusion. Rosemary enhances memory. A few drops, diffused into the air or dabbed on wrists while studying or writing, clears the mind and stimulates creative thinking and intuitive vision. This oil encourages practical thinking and aids in problem-solving on physical, emotional, and spiritual levels. Rosemary oil or incense are traditional aids for centering and focusing the mind on meditation.

Use of Rosemary oil is not recommended during pregnancy, in cases of epilepsy, or when fever is present.

THYME

Thyme is a bushy shrub with small green leaves and white flowers. Essential oil of Thyme is extracted both from leaves and flowers. There are more than 150 species of Thyme. The most powerful is Red Thyme, recognized by its orange or brown-red color. The recommended use in aromatherapy for Red Thyme is air diffusion, because of its high concentration of phenol, a strong skin irritant. A milder variety is Thyme Linalol, a pale yellow, thin liquid recommended for skin application diluted in a carrier oil or bathwater. Some manufacturers produce White

Thyme essential oil, a colorless oil which is a multi-distillation of Red Thyme and less irritating on the skin.

All varieties of Thyme smell the same to a degree, Red Thyme being the most intense. The aroma is spicy, sweet, woody, and slightly medicinal. Thyme oil was used in ancient Egypt, Rome and Greece in baths, burners, and as a massage oil and disinfectant to fill the atmosphere with its pleasing herbal fragrance. Thyme's effect is energizing, strengthening, purifying, and re-balancing.

Thyme is the major essential oil used to fight infection, either bacterial or viral. It aids in the production of white blood cells, strengthens the immune system, and helps fight colds, sore throat, and influenza. Thyme stimulates the production of red blood cells, thereby increasing oxygen throughout the body and bringing renewed vigor. It is used during illness to regulate a depressed appetite and improve sluggish digestion, and poor elimination (including constipation). This essential oil simultaneously enlivens and calms bodily systems, restoring strength and stamina, especially in cases of chronic fatigue and accompanying lack of sexual interest, frigidity, or impotence.

Essential oil of Thyme is useful in cases of lethargy, melancholia, and depression (including postpartum). For its grounding and re-balancing action, Thyme is used to treat mental spacey-ness, unrealistic thinking, and lack of motivation. Thyme gives a feeling of courage, determination, and resolve.

Avoid every variety of Thyme during pregnancy and in cases of high blood pressure.

- Red Thyme is not suitable for use in massage oil or bathwater, nor with children.

MEEMAW'S FAVORITES

BERGAMOT

ANTI-BIOTIC, DISINFECTANT, ANALGESIC, SEDATIVE,
CICATRISANT, ANTI-SPASMODIC, ANTI-SEPTIC, VULNERARY

Good for acne, abscesses, anxiety, boils, cold sores,
itching, oily skin, and psoriasis.

BIRCH

TONIC, DISINFECTANT, STIMULANT, ANALGESIC, DEPURATIVE,
ANTI-RHEUMATIC, ANTI-ARTHRITIC, DIURETIC, ANTI-SEPTIC,
ASTRINGENT, FEBRIFUGE, ANTI-BACTERIAL, DEPURATIVE

Known for reducing pain in the joints and muscles.
Also, an antispasmodic and relieves cramping
throughout the body.

BLACK PEPPER

ANALGESIC, CIRCULATORY, WARMING

Used for aching muscles, arthritis, detox, muscle
cramps, and poor circulation.

CARROT SEED

ANTI-SEPTIC, DISINFECTANT, ANALGESIC, DETOXIFIER, ANTI-OXIDANT, ANTI-CARCINOGENIC, DEPURATIVE, DIURETIC, STIMULANT, CYTOPHYLACTIC, TONIC, VERMIFUGE

Carrot oil acts on eczema, gout, mature skin, toxin build-up, and water retention. Carrot oil is full of anti-oxidants. Carotenoids boost the immune response to UV rays to prevent sun damage, stimulate skin cell rejuvenation, aid in the detoxification process, and help to heal chronic skin conditions like eczema and psoriasis.

CHAMOMILE (ROMAN)

ANALGESIC, SEDATIVE

Chamomile can soothe or help with abscesses, arthritis, boils, cuts, dermatitis inflamed skin, insect bites, rheumatism, sores, sprains, strains, and wounds.

CLARY SAGE

ANTI-CONVULSIVE, ANTI-SPASMODIC, ANTI-SEPTIC, ASTRINGENT, ANTI-BACTERIAL, DEODORANT, HYPOTENSIVE, NERVINE, SEDATIVE

Calming and soothing properties. Helps to ease muscle tension and spasms.

CLOVE

ANTI-MICROBIAL ANTI-FUNGAL, ANTI-SEPTIC, ANTI-VIRAL, STIMULANT

Recommended for skin care, especially for acne. It

can lessen wrinkles, sagging skin, and can rejuvenate the area around the eyes.
(DO NOT GET IN EYES)

CYPRESS OIL

ASTRINGENT, ANTI-SEPTIC, ANTI-SPASMODIC, CIRCULATORY, DEODORANT, DIURETIC, SUDORIFIC, VASOCONSTRICTOR, SEDATIVE

Cypress oil helps to improve circulation, strengthen skin, and reduce the appearance of varicose veins and broken capillaries under the skin's surface, immune system, helps to clear out cramps, stress, tension and swelling, great for sore muscles. Also used for excessive perspiration, oily skin, rheumatism, varicose veins.

ELEMI

ANTI-SEPTIC, ANALGESIC, STIMULANT, TONIC

Used for mature skin, scars, stress, and wounds.

EUCALYPTUS

ANALGESIC, ANTI-INFLAMMATORY, ANTI-SPASMODIC, DECONGESTANT, DEODORANT, ANTI-SEPTIC, ANTI-BACTERIAL, STIMULATING, CIRCULATORY, ANTI-INFLAMMATORY

Strengthen the immune system, protect skin health, ease tension and anxiety, eliminate inflammation, and fight against bacterial infection. Good for muscle pain and nerve pain, poor circulation, and cold sores.

FENNEL

ANTI-SEPTIC, ANTI-SPASMODIC, DEPURATIVE, DIURETIC, STIMULANT, STOMACHIC, TONIC, VERMIFUGE

Used for bruises, cellulite, obesity, toxin build-up, and water retention.

FRANKINCENSE

ANTI-SEPTIC, DISINFECTANT, ASTRINGENT, CICATRISANT, CYTOPHYLACTIC, DIURETIC, SEDATIVE, ANTI-SPASMODIC, ANALGESIC, WARMING

Helps with scars and stretch marks, and helps even out skin tone and helps get rid of sunspots and age spots. Astringent properties help protect skin cells. Reduces acne blemishes, the appearance of large pores and wrinkles. Reduces saggy skin like the abdomen, jowls, or under the eyes. It strengthens skin and improves its tone and elasticity. Used for healing dry or cracked skin and balancing skin's pH.

GERANIUM

ASTRINGENT, ANTI-BACTERIAL, ANTI-MICROBIAL, CICATRISANT, CYTOPHYLACTIC, VERMIFUGE, ANTI-INFLAMMATORY

Helps with irritation, improve the health of the skin, lightens age spots, and evens out overall skin tone. Geranium oil also improves circulation under the skins surface which aids in cell regeneration, making it useful for fading scars, wrinkles, and other visible imperfections in the skin. Helps with acne, cellulite, dull and oily skin.

GINGER

ANTI-SEPTIC, ANALGESIC, ANTI-INFLAMMATORY, STIMULATING

Provides relief from aching muscles and eases spasms in the muscles. Ginger supports muscles with its warming action together with its pain relieving properties. Use to treat arthritic and rheumatic pain, muscle pain and sprains.

GRAPEFRUIT

DIURETIC, DISINFECTANT, STIMULANT, ANTI-SEPTIC, TONIC

Known for helping with cellulite, dull skin, toxin build-up, and water retention.

JUNIPER BERRY

ANTI-SEPTIC, ANTI-RHEUMATIC, ANTI-SPASMODIC, ASTRINGENT, DEPURATIVE, DIURETIC, RUBEFACIENT, SUDORIFIC, STIMULANT, TONIC, VULNERARY

Helps with cellulite, gout, rheumatism, and toxin build-up. Relieves nerve pain, joint and muscle aches and spasms.

HELICHRYSUM

ANTI-SPASMODIC, ANTI-COAGULANT, ANTI-ALLERGENIC, ANTI-MICROBIAL, NERVINE, ANTI-INFLAMMATORY, CICATRISANT, FEBRIFUGE, ANTI-SEPTIC, EMOLLIENT, ANTI-FUNGAL, DIURETIC, CYTOPHYLACTIC, ANALGESIC

Used to treat abscesses, acne, burns, cuts, dermatitis, eczema, irritations, and wounds. Helps to relieve arthritis pain and supports the nerves.

LAVENDER

ANTI-INFLAMMATORY, ANTI-INFLAMMATORY, ANTI-MICROBIAL, SEDATIVE, ANALGESIC, ANTI-OXIDANT

Relieve stress, improve mood, and promotes restful sleep. Helps with acne, athlete's foot, bruises, burns, cuts, dermatitis, headache, itching, oily skin, rheumatism, scars, sores, sprains, strains, stress, and stretch marks.

MARJORAM

ANALGESIC, ANTI-SPASMODIC, ANTI-SEPTIC, ANTI-VIRAL, ANTI-BACTERIAL, CORDIAL, DIAPHORETIC, DIURETIC, ANTI-FUNGAL, HYPOTENSIVE, NERVINE, SEDATIVE, VASODILATOR, VULNERARY, CIRCULATORY

Warming, soothing, and antispasmodic properties help to ease joint pain and muscle spasms.

MELISSA

CORDIAL, NERVINE, SEDATIVE, ANTI-SPASMODIC, ANTI-BACTERIAL, DIAPHORETIC, FEBRIFUGE, HYPOTENSIVE, SUDORIFIC, TONIC

Melissa can help with herpes, shingles, and cold sores, but it is most used to soothe.

MYRRH

ANTI-MICROBIAL ANTI-VIRAL, ASTRINGENT, ANTI-FUNGAL, STIMULANT, DIAPHORETIC, VULNERARY, ANTI-SEPTIC, IMMUNE BOOSTER, CIRCULATORY, TONIC, ANTI-INFLAMMATORY

Boosts skin strength for a smooth and healthy complexion. Can help with athlete's foot, chapped skin, itching, and ringworm. Helps to fade away scars and spots, good for treating skin ailments and skin diseases like eczema, ringworm, and itching.

NEROLI OIL

ANTI-SEPTIC, ANTI-BACTERIAL, ANTI-INFLAMMATORY, ANTI-SEPTIC, CORDIAL, EMOLLIENT, SEDATIVE, TONIC, CICATRISANT, CYTOPHYLACTIC, DISINFECTANT, ANTI-SPASMODIC

Good for mature skin, oily skin, scars, stretch marks. It makes the skin smooth, free from infections and adds a healthy glow. It also helps to maintain the right moisture and oil balance in the skin and promotes the generation of new cells.

ORANGE

ANTI-INFLAMMATORY, ANTI-SPASMODIC, ANTI-SEPTIC, DIURETIC, TONIC, SEDATIVE

Relaxes muscular and nervous spasms, relieves inflammation, inhibits the growth of bacteria in wounds. Its use as a tonic keeps the metabolic system in proper shape, contributes to strength, and boosts immunity.

OREGANO

ANTI-OXIDANT, ANTI-BACTERIAL, STIMULATING

Famous for its effect on immune health. Reduces oxidative stress and defends the body against a wide range of bacteria.

PEPPERMINT

ANALGESIC, NERVINE

Beneficial for muscle and joint pain, headache, fever, and nerve pain.

ROSEMARY

TONIC, ANTI-INFLAMMATORY, ANTI-SEPTIC, ANTI-BACTERIAL, ANTI-SPASMODIC, ANALGESIC, IMMUNE BOOSTER, STIMULANT CIRCULATORY, DETOXIFIER

Known for soothing aching muscles, arthritis, dull skin, exhaustion, muscle cramping, neuralgia, poor circulation, and rheumatism. Good for relieving back pain, muscle and joint pain and headaches. Helps to tighten skin, reducing the appearance of fine lines and wrinkles, and can be applied topically to a wide variety of ailments, including reducing cellulite, improving hair growth, and healing skin.

SPRUCE

ANTI-ARTHRITIC, ANTI-RHEUMATIC, ANTISPASMODIC, CICATRISANT, CIRCULATORY, DECONGESTANT, DETOXIFIER, EMOLLIENT, INSECTICIDE, ANTI-PARASITIC, VULNERARY

Helps cure arthritis and rheumatism by improving blood circulation, treats muscular spasms. Diminishes scars from acne, pimples, or a pox on the skin. This oil speeds up the growth of new tissues and cells in the affected area, rejuvenates aging skin, good for healing wounds and is used to treat abscesses, acne, and boils because of its detoxifying properties.

SWEET MARJORAM

SEDATIVE, ANALGESIC, ANTI-SPASMODIC, ANTI-RHEUMATIC

Helps to relieve muscle pain and spasms, stiffness, rheumatism, osteoarthritis, and migraine. Relieves aching muscles, arthritis, cramps, migraine, neuralgia, rheumatism, spasm, and sprains.

TEA TREE

ANTI-BACTERIAL, ANTI-MICROBIAL, ANTI-SEPTIC, ANTI-VIRAL, CICATRISANT, ANTI-FUNGAL, INSECTICIDE, STIMULANT, SUDORIFIC

Heals wounds quickly and protects them from infections. Fades scar marks and after spots left by eruptions, boils, pox, and acne. It can be applied directly on the wounds, boils, sores, cuts or certain eruptions, including insect bites and stings, to protect from infections.

THYME

ANTI-SPASMODIC, ANALGESIC, HYPOTENSIVE, CIRCULATORY

Boosts the immune system, protect against chronic diseases, stimulates blood flow, prevent fungal infections, and relieves stress. Known for helping with arthritis, cuts, and dermatitis. Good for joint and muscle pain, effective for aches and pains caused by over exercising or sports injuries.

VETIVER

ANTI-INFLAMMATORY, ANTI-SEPTIC, APHRODISIAC, CICATRISANT, NERVINE, SEDATIVE, TONIC, VULNERARY

Brings relief to general aches and pains, especially for rheumatism, arthritis and muscular pain and headache. Also good for acne and oily skin.

YLANG-YLANG

ANTI-SEBORRHOEIC, ANTI-SEPTIC, HYPOTENSIVE, NERVINE, SEDATIVE

Known to regularize sebum production and help with seborrheic eczema. Helps wounds from becoming infected and helps avoid both sepsis and tetanus by inhibiting microbial growth and disinfecting wounds. Speeds up the healing of wounds.

GENERAL SAFETY PRECAUTIONS

The following suggested precautions are not a complete safety reference for essential oils. If you have any questions, please consult your physician or a trained aromatherapist.

A safe rule of thumb is to never use an essential oil undiluted on skin. Exceptions can be made for Lavender and Tea Tree oils, but only after careful experimentation with test patches. Some people might be hyper-sensitive even to Lavender and Tea Tree, the two gentlest essential oils.

- A skin patch test should be administered before every first-time use of an essential oil.
- Essential oils should only be taken internally under the supervision of a licensed medical practitioner.
- Essential oils are highly flammable. Use extreme care around fire.
- In the event of eye injury from the essential oil, irrigate the eye with a sterile, isotonic, saline solution for 15 minutes. Immediately

consult a physician if pain persists after the eyewash.

- Keep essential oils in a locked cabinet, away from children.
- Asthma and epilepsy patients should avoid Fennel, Hyssop, and Rosemary.
- Babies and elderly people require lower doses of essential oils, half what is recommended for a healthy adult. Peppermint and Eucalyptus have been known to cause respiratory problems with these age groups. Lavender and Neroli, despite their gentle nature, can be tolerated only in minute amounts (1 drop in bathwater and 1/2 drop an ounce of carrier oil.)
- Cancer patients may use mild dilutions of Bergamot, Chamomile, Lavender, Ginger and Frankincense.
- Persons undergoing chemotherapy should avoid using essential oils, especially Fennel and Aniseed.
- High blood pressure patients should avoid essential oils of Black Pepper, Clove, Hyssop, Peppermint, Rosemary, Sage, and Thyme.
- Low blood pressure patients should avoid excessive use of Lavender oil.
- Persons allergic to nuts cannot use Sweet Almond or peanut carrier oils. Safer alternatives are Sunflower, Canola (non-GM) and Safflower oils.
- Pregnant women should avoid essential oils before the 18th week of pregnancy, especially in cases of prior miscarriage. In

the second trimester, essential oils may be used in low doses formulated by a professional aromatherapist or health care provider.

- Beware of getting in the eyes or on mucous membranes (lips and genitals).
- If your muscles are extremely sore don't expect the pain to subside after a single essential oil massage application. You might have to give yourself a few day's rest before you recover.
- Do not use on open wounds

None of the information gathered here is meant as medical advice. Please see your doctor with any concerns.

If you're going to walk on thin ice, you might as well dance. —Meemaw Crone

Two wrongs are only the beginning.
—Meemaw Crone

In one ear and out the other. Take that with a grain of salt. —Meemaw Crone

OTHER ANECDOTAL USES

SLEEP

Keep the dream alive. Hit the snooze button. Having a fully restful night's sleep is important for your body and mind. Unsettled sleep will increase stress and tax your immune system, making you susceptible to disease and illnesses. Having a good night's sleep is similar to recharging your body's batteries to make it most efficient for the next day. Poor sleeping habits can inefficiently relieve stress leaving it to damage your body and mind.

Getting six to seven hours of sleep is important for your body to replenish the energy levels that it has lost from the day's activities. However, sleeping a quality six hours of sleep is more valuable than sleeping a poor, restless ten hours of sleep.

Always practice good sleep hygiene. This includes no caffeine in the evenings, no spicy meals, and eating until uncomfortable. Also consider not using a phone, tablet, or computer to read before bed, unless the emitted light can be adjusted to an evening hue.

Take a warm bath, practice meditation, listen to soft music, or do other relaxing activities in the evenings. Yoga may be a good choice to relax the muscles in the evening but avoid vigorous exercise.

Avoid alcohol before bedtime.

Essential oils used in aromatherapy can help you relax to help you fall into a deep sleep. You will notice the difference the next morning when you wake up and feel revitalized from the previous day. Not only will you feel restored on the outside, your mind and body will be healthier from a quality night's sleep.

The most relaxing of all the essential oils are Bergamot, Sage, and Sandalwood. Although each has helpful results, combining all three has the best effect on your mind and body.

BERGAMOT

Bergamot is a peel from an exotic fruit that smells like citrus. The potent smell makes you feel refreshed and calms your emotions. Blend Bergamot with other oils and use in a diffuser, or mix with carrier oils and massage into tense muscles.

CLARY SAGE

Clary Sage relaxes your spirit and gets rid of the restlessness from stress and excess emotions. It brings a feeling of well-being.

SANDALWOOD AGMARK

Sandalwood is great for soothing the mind on stressful restless nights.

Although each of these brings a distinct benefit, they are most helpful used together. Buy the essential oils separately or use them in combination. Combining the oils will guarantee good sleep and a refreshed morning.

Other essential oils specifically used for sleep include Cedarwood, Ylang-Ylang, Vetiver Chamomile, Lavender, and Marjoram.

My fondest memories are of gardening with Fat Mammy, my great grandma. We would hold seeds in our hands and pray to God for him to bless them, then blow life into them and say, 'live in Jesus name!' If any of the seeds didn't sprout in our hands immediately we tossed them away because they were dead. Most would respond and break through their seed shells showing tender young plants. Our garden was always good and productive. As long as God blesses we shall never starve. —Granny Deedra

RELAXATION

Relaxation is an important part of a daily regimen. Most people focus on daily work schedules, exercise, home care, taking care of children, and other personal chores for daily living. Most people ignore the importance of relaxation and rest. Resting the mind and body helps refresh energy and brings back a balance of body strength and fortitude.

Relaxation essential oils also induce a mindful state of calm that helps you forget chores and stress. Relaxation does not mean sleep. Relaxation guides your mind away from stressful thoughts and into a peaceful state. Relaxation soothes your whole body and reduces the tiring effects of stress.

Although the goal for relaxation methods is to calm and create a sense of peace, they do not make you tired. Using essential oils in the office will give you peace throughout the day and help you maintain your temper during high-stress moments.

Several essential oils can help you relax in your home or office. Essential oils like Ylang-Ylang,

Chamomile, and Neroli will help you relax without making you tired. Each has their own unique impact, but when used together they help you feel at peace.

In the office, you may not be able to use a diffuser. Meemaw suggests wearing a pendant, with a few drops of whatever smells good to you.

YLANG-YLANG

Ylang-Ylang is a potent essential oil that is sensual and relaxing. The balancing influence from the exotic aroma leaves your whole body and spirit feeling relaxed. It is also a romantic aroma and it is perfect for date night or cuddling.

CHAMOMILE MAROC

Chamomile Maroc is one of the most popular soothing aromas. It will combat irritability and anger from a stressful day. If you are a person who has anger issues, this is one oil that can help you calm down.

NEROLI

Neroli has a combination of relaxation actions that restore your peace while rejuvenating your overall energy and body strength. Neroli is an exotic plant that has a deep influence on emotions. The fragrance can reduce stress and disperse the anger left in your body.

All of these oils will help you throughout your day even if used individually. Used together, they remove the heavy emotional response to stress and tension. Removing the negative impact of the day can help maintain balance, and help with anger management. You will find yourself more productive, with a better attitude. Use these essential oils in combination with other stress relieving oils and you will find your whole presence to be more positive.

When something went very wrong, my Papaw would say that 'Lightning just hit the shit house.' —Mamaw Crank

I'm busier than a cat tryin' to cover crap on a marble floor. —Auntie Rae

Enemas cure everything. —Mama Kay

FIGHT DEPRESSION

Depression can hit you at any point of your life, but it is common later in life due to changes in the brain. Some are chronically disabled from depression since childhood. It is important to do something to help boost your self-esteem and rid your life from depression. Depression can cause anxiety and it can ultimately cause you to become unhealthy and physically harm your body.

Depression comes in different varieties, from rare outbreaks caused by grief or other setbacks to long-term disability with seemingly no external factors.

Aromatherapy is a natural way to help you balance mood swings and deal with debilitating depression. Some people use drugs and other chemicals with known side-effects, desperate to ease their suffering.

Not only is depression bad for your mental health, but it can affect your physical health. Depression can cause stress, a killer for people who keep emotions inside. Depression can cause social anxiety and health issues. It can be the cause of a loss of appetite, mood swings, family tension, and job loss.

Other natural ways to aid in reducing depression is daily exercise, eating fresh fruits and vegetables, and a boost in self-confidence. Essential oils can help you fight off depression effectively without all the drugs and chemicals. Aromatherapy penetrates the senses and helps fight off the negative effects of depression with stimulating fragrances and scents.

The following are powerful solutions to help fight off depression. Jasmine, Lavender, and Neroli will boost your mood and help balance your emotions. Use each of these separately for their individual benefits to help you fight depression. Use them together as a potent solution to help fight depression.

JASMINE

Jasmine is a sensual essential oil that helps you assert yourself. It can relax you after the stressful day and it can lift your emotions. It can also boost your confidence and self-esteem to help overcome obstacles.

LAVENDER FRENCH

Lavender French is a soothing essential oil that can help you mentally relax. It is an herb from France that has become popular for its therapeutic uses. It can balance your mood and release tension from mind and muscles.

NEROLI

Neroli is a popular relaxing and rejuvenating essential oil. Its fragrance is incredibly relaxing and it can help you dispel anger and irritability.

Other essential oils known to help with depression include Bergamot, Chamomile, Clary Sage, Frankincense, Geranium, Grapefruit, Helichrysum, Lemon, Mandarin, Palo Santo, Orange, Rose, Sandalwood, and Ylang-Ylang.

You gotta learn how to separate the fly shit from the pepper. —Granny Bop

Washing your hair while on your period will make you cramp harder. Going outside with wet hair will give you a deathly cold. —Grandma Loretta

Shit fire and save the matches!!!!
—Mamaw Crone

FIGHT LONELINESS

If you are single and live alone, the feelings of loneliness can start to creep up on you. Loneliness often leads to depression, social anxiety, and undue stress. Fight back with therapeutic scents and fragrances, and get a boost in emotional balance.

Many people spend more time online which can lead to loneliness. Holding in emotions is a required part of a professional attitude. Unfortunately, it can lead to depression or an emotionally unbalanced behavior pattern. The essential oils will release these internal feelings and help you relax your mind.

The following essential oils will help you battle loneliness. They can be used individually, but are better in combination for their synergistic effect for soothing anxiety. Marjoram Sweet and Rosemary are both powerful essential oils to use in the office or at home to relieve you of mental worry and loneliness.

MARJORAM SWEET

Marjoram Sweet is a naturally soothing and comforting oil that can help release your anxiety and increase your mood. The herb is a culinary herb used for many centuries as an herbal medicine. It is a powerful mood enhancer, and it can help you overcome your feelings of loneliness and depression. Another effect that Marjoram Sweet can bring is a warm, sweet fragrance that helps your aching muscles. Try it in a carrier oil and massage it into your muscles.

ROSEMARY

Rosemary has long been used to help people relieve themselves from the pressures and stress of the day. If you suffer from loneliness, stress and anxiety can make your mental health worse. Rosemary can also increase your memory and enable you to deal with the ups and downs of anxiety and depression that stems from loneliness. Rosemary rejuvenates tired muscles and helps ease the aches and pains from a strenuous day's work.

Using each of these essential oils will benefit your emotional state and help you deal with the pressures of loneliness. Try using aromatherapy in your home and office to increase your mood and deal with emotional pressure.

Other essential oils known to suppress loneliness include Clary Sage, Frankincense, Helichrysum, Palo Santo, Roman Chamomile, Rose, Frankincense, Clary Sage, and Bergamot.

FIGHT SADNESS

Sadness can stem from the loss of a loved one, finances, job disappointment, or even from stress or worry. Sadness cuts into the soul and causes our bodies to become ill, increasing hormones which can weaken your immune system.

Another complication with sadness is that it can eventually lead to deep depression. Depression is a scary place for anyone who has suffered from the disease. Depression can lead to emotional ups and downs making it difficult to stay calm at work, deal with stress, and live a fulfilling life. Sadness that leads to depression can be helped with aromatherapy.

Aromatherapy can help you fight the emotional roots of sadness. Diffusing essential oils in your office will lighten your mood and help ward off bad emotions, keeping you calm and balanced. Essential oils will help you become more productive and even create a better work environment. It can also help you better communicate with co-workers, your bosses, and provide better customer service.

Burning a tiny few drops at home can enhance your mood and overall health. Try an oil-burning candle holder, or a plug-in wax burner.

Beating sadness is hard if you are a stay-at-home mom or homemaker who spends many hours alone. Aromatherapy can cheer mood and keep you calm when the kids are acting up or chores become overwhelming. Being over emotional ruins the day.

Bergamot and Neroli are essential oils can help you fight sadness and rid yourself from depression. It is important to use them when you feel emotions becoming negative. Even better, use the oils several times a week to help prevent sadness from developing. Bergamot and Neroli can enhance your mood and keep you uplifted. Use them individually for their separate positive components, or use them synergistically for a powerful mood enhancer.

BERGAMOT

Bergamot is a powerfully uplifting essential oil that can refresh your spirit. If you are having negative thoughts and feel like you are feeling depressed or sad, Bergamot can help soothe your mind. Bergamot is extracted from the peel of a fruit, so it has an understandably citrus smell. The citrus smell refreshes the mind and helps put you in a better mood which will ultimately reduce sadness.

NEROLI

Neroli is one of the best essential oils to relax your mind. It is perfect with Bergamot since it can follow up with a relaxing feel after ridding yourself from sadness. It is also distilled from a flower from the Bitter Orange tree. The fragrance helps soothe your mind to help it relax. It is especially helpful to give you better sleep. It rids your mind of anger, sadness, and the irritability of the day.

Other essential oils known for combatting sadness include Ylang-Ylang, Lavender, Clary Sage, and Frankincense.'

Never use a hatchet to remove a fly from your friend's forehead. —Meemaw Crone

The sooner you fall behind, the more time you'll have to catch up. —Meemaw Crone

He who seeks revenge should remember to dig two graves. —Meemaw Crone

HELP COPE WITH GRIEF

In a blink of an eye, grief hits us fast and unexpectedly. It is one of the hardest emotions to release, and it never leaves you spiritually. It can be the impact from the loss of a loved one, family troubles, or even the loss of a job. Aromatherapy can relieve the stress and pain from all of these sources. Bereavement is a strong emotional pain that can overcome your life. It stays with you for a lifetime. Bereavement is painful and can interfere with your relationships, home life, and employment.

To fight against grief is to help cope with feelings. Grief can create a feeling of loss that can kill your soul and build tension in muscles. It will eventually cause you to lose your health, and become sick or ill from emotional stress. Illnesses from grief are not uncommon, especially with the loss of a loved one.

Using the below essential oils will help you maintain a healthier attitude towards life and increase your confidence for future endeavors. Your mental health is more important than you might realize. It can control your physical health, and a downward spiral of depression can ultimately lead to tragic events. Using Frankincense and Rose can help you boost your mood and keep your mind balanced from the overwhelming emotions from grief.

FRANKINCENSE

Frankincense is a rejuvenating essential oil that can help you balance strong emotions that come with the negative impact of grief. It is an exotic plant extracted from a bush in Africa. Frankincense is an essential oil used for thousands of years as a therapeutic ingredient to help people relax, and to aid in meditation. It was also used in ancient religious ceremonies to uplift the spirit and help the mood.

ROSE

Rose is a unique essential oil that helps balance the mind and relax your spirit and muscles. It is undoubtedly a feminine oil that makes you feel sensual and soft. Its influence on the emotional system uplifts and balances your mood. Stabilizing your mood is especially important for those who suffer from grief, so this is an emotional solution.

Although feelings of loss and grief cannot be eliminated, aromatherapy can elevate your mood and balance your emotions to help you deal with the issues and overcome the depression that accompanies grief. Use both of these essential oils for help with grief. Use them individually for their separate benefits. Use it to overcome grief so depression does not overcome your mind and spirit. Take the journey to feeling better.

Other essential oils known to help with grief include Sandalwood, Lavender, Cedarwood, Mandarin, Neroli, Cypress, Helichrysum, Palo Santo, Vetiver, Ylang-Ylang, and Jasmine.

It's not the fall that hurts, it's the landing.
—Meemaw Crone

If a younger sibling marries before you do, it's said he or she made you dance in the hog trough. —Mam Vickie

If there's enough blue sky to knit a cat a sweater, then you'd have fair weather.
—Mamaw Annie

Shit in one hand and wish in the other, see which one fills up faster. —Mom-Mom

Learn from the mistakes of others. You can't live long enough to make them all yourself.
—Meemaw Crone

FIGHT APATHY

Apathy has become a major issue in society. As individuals, we are constantly bombarded with negativity from work, home, or even a simple outing. We are handed stress-related issues in our lives and after a time we can become apathetic to even the most important aspects of our lives. Being apathetic only serves to worsen your mood and it can make you feel spiritually down.

Using essential oils can enhance your mood and help you battle against those apathetic feelings. Apathy is a downward spiral for any professional especially if you own your own business. Someone having an incredibly bad day needs to relieve the pressures of the day.

Increased apathy eventually leads to increased levels of stress, lowering energy and harming your health. Nothing good comes from apathy, so focusing on exercise and increasing your mood will benefit you in all aspects of your life. Aromatherapy will help increase your mood and make you feel more refreshed.

Use essential oils in your home or office. When used in your office, apathy seems to fade away even during stressful times. Essential oils are not only safe and effective, but they are a natural way to rid your body of harmful emotional toxins. Essential oils used in the office as a pleasant scent throughout the day will help to keep your emotional stress levels at bay so you will be at the best performance possible for your coworkers and customers.

Use essential oil in aromatherapy for the home to help you and your family members wind down from the day or keep spirits high for visitors. The aromatherapy is safe for your children, and the sweet scents can be enjoyed by all ages. Even children go through tough times and they too can be affected by apathy. Using essential oils in the home can help all your family members fight off apathy and provide them with a happier, healthier lifestyle.

The following essential oils can be used individually for their respective benefits. Used in combination, these essential oils can be a potent eliminator of harmful emotions.

BASIL

Basil is a strengthening herb that can free you from emotional constraints. Basil is a powerful essential oil that helps you spiritually clear your mind, and it gives you clarity to concentrate more effectively. Basil has a long track record of having natural medicinal purposes that date back to ancient history.

GRAPEFRUIT

Grapefruit is a popular combination with other essential oils for its refreshing fragrance that improves moods and boosts energy levels. The citrus smell helps wake you up from the night's sleep and gives you the energy to tackle the day.

PEPPERMINT

Peppermint is known for its cool, refreshing scent that clears your thoughts and opens your mind. It aids in your overall concentration, so it is a good essential oil for your office or home during the day. Peppermint has an everlasting soothing effect, and it can be used in burners or even a bath to alleviate stress and relieve any aches and pains. Peppermint is a powerful essential oil for adult use only.

While each of these oils can benefit you individually, the combination will quickly remove negative thoughts and help set up a positive attitude. Essential oils are a safe, effective way to remove the apathy from your daily life. As apathy leaves your emotions, you will find yourself in a better state of mind and you may even see your own health increase. Improving your mood can also help keep your relationships healthy and keep you emotionally stable.

Other essential oils that can fight apathy and fatigue include Rose, Lavender, Rosemary, Lemon,

Bergamot, Frankincense, and Sandalwood. Other essential oils known to help enhance mood include Black Pepper, Clary Sage, Cypress, Ginger, Helichrysum, Jasmine, Patchouli, Vetiver, Orange, Ylang-Ylang, Rose, and Chamomile.

If you can't remember what you were going to say, well, it must have been a lie.
—Grammy Hollis

You're better off runnin' through hell with gasoline drawers than to fuck with me.
—Granny Puck

You'll look like hell if you don't get a good night's sleep. —Granma Wheeler

IRRITABILITY RELIEF

Irritability can happen for many reasons from negative energy. Irritability is an emotional issue that develops from a bad day or over a longer period. Some people have the ability to hold in their anger, but the emotional irritability caused by negative reactions can bubble to the surface and cause even the most even-tempered person to finally respond with anger.

Aromatherapy can increase your body's ability to defend and fight back against the emotional negativity of irritability. Irritability stems from several issues that occur throughout the day. Deadlines at work, the pressure of the day's work, and any other stressful event can cause a person to suffer from irritability. Irritability can also stem from home related issues. Stay-at-home moms also suffer from irritability of deadlines, taking care of the kids, and making sure everything in the household is perfect.

Aromatherapy can help you resolve your irritability issues and they can help calm you for future work days. Even as your environment changes, essential oils will help you quell irritability that can cause a negative response. Once you use essential oils for irritability relief, you will start to notice how your attitude changes. You may even see how people will respond to you differently once your attitude has changed to a more positive attitude.

Change in living conditions or economic status can also cause irritability. With poor economic stability, it is hard to hold a positive attitude. Using essential oils can preserve emotional control even during tragedy. Although misfortune should be nurtured emotionally, it can be a base cause for irritability in your life. The aroma from essential oils can help calm your nerves and bring you a positive attitude even on the low days.

The following essential oils are the perfect way to release stress and bring calm to your irritability. Chamomile, Lavender, and Neroli are the three primary essential oils that bring calm to your body and mind. Use separately or combine them for a potent mix of powerful oils that will remove your irritability almost instantly.

CHAMOMILE MAROC

Chamomile Maroc is a soothing and relaxing essential oil. It is the first step in removing the negative influence of the day. The essential oil is a great way to control your anger and keep your emotional system at a defined balance. The irritation from the day will disappear as this scent soothes your head and mind.

LAVENDER FRENCH

Lavender French is a popular essential oil to help rejuvenated your otherwise bruised emotional mind. The essential oil comes from Europe, but it is mostly cultivated from France. It has been well-known to have therapeutic results that can help increase health and increase your energy. By removing the tension from your muscles and mind, you limit irritability.

NEROLI

The Neroli essential oil will allow tension release and a relaxing feeling. It is derived from the bitter Orange tree and distilled into a rejuvenating essential oil. Relaxation dispels anger and helps lift your mood.

Each of these essential oils is revitalizing even without the combination. However, using them in combination can create a potent effect to deal with emotional issues and remove the irritability that can bring more stress into your life.

Other essential oils that help with irritability are Mandarin, Roman Chamomile, and Sandalwood.

Don't borrow trouble. —Granny Grunt

Ask the Lord for help. Put on your big girl drawers, and do what has to be done.
—Maw Maw Up the Road

Dreading it is worse than doing it. Can't never could do nothing, but I do anyway. —Mama Bob

Always remember you're unique. Just like everyone else. —Meemaw Crone

REDUCE STRESS

Reducing stress is one of the major afflictions that most people try to reduce in their daily lives. Stress is a contributing cause to disease in busy people who do not relieve their bodies of the stress that accumulates throughout the day. Essential oils used in aromatherapy help reduce the stress levels and keep you healthier and happier during the day and in your overall life.

Stress is the number one killer of people under the age of 40. Even if your stress levels are under control, benefit by lowering stress further with essential oils. The health benefits alone are worth your while to try aromatherapy. It is a non-evasive way to reduce stress and relax your mind so to sleep better and relax during times when emotions may get the best of you.

Essential oils are a good way to balance your stress and give your body an emotional overhaul. Use essential oils at work to reduce stress as it increases throughout the day. Your work environment is probably the most stressful part of your day, so using essential oils in your office can help calm and relax you during your workday. Office aromatherapy is a vital positive therapy for your body and mind, especially during busy days.

Even if you don't go to a corporate job, a home life can also be stressful. Keeping essential oils in your home using aromatherapy can keep the stress of keeping a clean, proper home at low levels. Essential oils are harmless to children, so keep the aroma from the essential oils burning throughout your home without harming any family members.

Several essential oils are used to reduce stress. Although each of the following oils has their individual benefits, combine them for an overall high level of therapy for your stress levels. Helpful essential oils are Basil, Juniper Berry, and Geranium. A second combination that is equally useful is a mixture of Chamomile Maroc, Lavender French, and Sandalwood Agmark.

BASIL

Basil can help clear the mind from stress and strengthen body and spirit. It brings clarity to your mind that is good for your daily chores. Basil is an ancient therapy used to revive personal well-being and emotional peace. Basil can make you feel strong throughout the day, and can keep your body maintained with an overall mindful awareness of your emotions keeping them in check.

JUNIPER BERRY

Juniper berry is a strong scent that fortifies the mind and body. It is a distilled berry from a Juniper tree that brings the pungent and effective fragrance. Juniper berry is also a well-known fragrance that can expel and clear toxins from your body's system and it soothes the muscles and joints.

GERANIUM

Geranium helps stabilize your body and mind bringing a balance of emotions and stress levels. Its nurturing fragrance makes you feel as if you have removed all the bad in life and expelled it from your body. It is especially worthwhile to those who feel like their emotions are a roller coaster and out of control. It has a flowery scent and it blends with almost any of the other essential oils.

Although each of these essential oils is highly effective individually, using them in combination can increase your ability to remove stress and help your body heal from the emotional drama. Although essential aroma aromatherapy is not a perfect solution, it can give your body release from stress and harmful emotions. Give these combinations a try and you will notice a difference within a few days. Use them in the office and you will notice your attitude towards people and life itself will turn to a positive outlook.

Anything is possible if you don't know what you are talking about. —Meemaw Crone

A man with both feet firmly on the ground is a man who can't get his pants off.
—Meemaw Crone

The nail that sticks up above the rest will get hammered down first. —Meemaw Crone

RELIEVE DEBILITATING STRESS

The stress from work, home life, schedules, and other deadlines can cause undue stress. Stress is reported to be an extremely exhausting emotional state that harms your mental and physical health. Some people rely on drugs or other substance to help cure the stress in their everyday lives. Stress can be relieved through essential oils treatments, by using drops in the bath or diffuser, or mixing with a carrier oil and massaging into the skin.

The stress that affects many people affects their emotional state and can cause severe depression and low self-esteem. The low self-esteem that afflicts people can limit their work productivity, cause social anxiety, and ruin home life. Low self-esteem can also be seen by your children when you come home for the day. Overall, it can take an increased toll on your mental health, physical health, and social relationships with friends and family.

Low self-esteem can be reversed through effective aromatherapy. Use the essential oils in your office to help boost your mood and rid yourself from the stress that accompanies low self-esteem. The essential oils will increase your confidence and counteract the negative influence of low self-esteem.

Essential oils can also be used in your home. They can help you manage the stress and relax your mind from the hectic schedules and deadlines. Aromatherapy can reduce low self-esteem inhibiting your success. If you suffer from the negative influence of low self-esteem, essential oils can help you fight back.

The following essential oils for aromatherapy can be used individually or in combination. Used in combination, they are powerful therapeutic ways of ridding your body from the stress and tension from the day. After a few drops burned, you will start to notice your mood boost and it will help relieve you from debilitating low self-esteem. Use Sandalwood Agmark and Ylang-Ylang for an emotional balance and mood enhancer.

SANDALWOOD AGMARK

Sandalwood Agmark is an important essential oil that will help relax and soothe your mind and body. It is a woody fragrance like being outside in a rugged forest. It will settle your mind from the low self-esteem and boost your confidence.

YLANG-YLANG

Ylang-Ylang is an exotic essential oil that is sensual and balances overactive emotions. It helps you spiritually, so your mind will be more positive after using Ylang-Ylang. It can also be used as a mood enhancer for romance and love.

The above essential oils will help you battle your low self-esteem. Everyone deserves a positive attitude towards life, and aromatherapy can help you realize your self-worth. Having a mood enhancer will better your home life and help you cope with the busy work schedule and deadlines.

Not only is it good for you to help fight low self-esteem, it is also important to help your body relax from the stress it causes. Stress is a killer for many people, so your body will thank you for the stress relief. Using aromatherapy will help you fight back and give you the life you deserve.

Other stress-relieving oils not included in the last two sections are Benzoin, Bergamot, Clary Sage, Frankincense, Grapefruit, Jasmine, Lavender, Mandarin, Neroli, Palo Santo, Patchouli, Roman Chamomile, Rose, Vetiver, Ginger, Cardamom, Eucalyptus, Orange, and Lemon.

Don't lift your arms over your head when pregnant. The cord could strangle the baby.
—Mawmaw Betty

My Auntie could look at how a woman was carrying a baby and tell the sex.
—Mamaw Dunning

When the baby is a few days old, grab the baby by its heels with its head hanging down. Shake his liver loose. If you don't, he'll be colicky.
—Nana Ruth

If you're not living on the edge, you're taking up too much room. —Meemaw Crone

Don't burn your candle from both ends.
—Meemaw Crone

REDUCE ANXIETY

Anxiety can inflict its horrible symptoms on people of any age. Anxiety comes in all different forms including family worries, panic attacks, or simply an inability to cope with the stress and hectic schedule of a busy work day. Anxiety raising the heart rate, causes mental fatigue, and it is overall dangerous to one's physical health. Some people will choose to see a therapist and use drugs or other chemicals to help rid themselves from daily anxiety. Some of these drugs have unknown side-effects, and it can cause future health problems. Using essential oil in relaxing ways can relieve stress, calm nerves, and help with sleep. Try using a few drops in bath oil, or mix with a carrier oil and massage in the skin.

Anxiety can stem from multiple places in our lives. Work environments with strict deadlines are places that foster worry, stress, and mental fatigue. The anxiety caused from these places can cause you to have problems concentrating and being efficient at your job. It can cause you to be sick more often than usual.

Poor relationships can also cause anxiety. If your relationship is failing or you suspect adultery, worrying and focusing on the negative can make you ultra-stressed. Essential oils can help soothe and relax your mind from all the negative and help you worry less. Worrying about a failing relationship can also harm your physical health, so using aromatherapy can help keep your body strong and relieve the stress from the day.

If you find yourself crippled by anxiety, essential oils can lift your spirits and help you fight back. Regaining control of your emotions can be done without the need of drugs and chemicals. The drugs used to treat mental issues can cloud your mind and alter your personality negatively. Essential oils are naturally relaxing methods to help you battle the anxiety and stress that plague you. Burning a few drops of essential oils can help you clear your mind from the clouded behavior.

The following essential oils are great ways to eliminate the stress in your life. Bergamot, Cedarwood, and Lavender are three essential oils that are important for proper meditation and anxiety elimination. They can be used individually for their separate benefits, but it is recommended to use them in combination. Used in combination, the essential oils can create a potent solution to debilitating anxiety and daily stress.

BERGAMOT

Bergamot is a refreshing and uplifting essential oil. It is extracted from the peel of the fruit, and its citrus aroma helps lift you spiritually and rid yourself of negative thoughts. It balances emotions and keeps you focused on important issues.

CEDARWOOD

Cedarwood is a soothing essential oil that helps remove stress from body and mind. The oil is extracted from the Virginian Cedar tree, so its fragrance is woody and refreshing to the mind.

LAVENDER FRENCH

Lavender French is one of the most popular flowery scents that rejuvenate your mind. The scent is French-born and it has long been considered a therapeutic fragrance. It relieves stress from your mind, and it can even reduce the aches and pains from your muscles.

Other essential oils known to reduce anxiety include Neroli, Geranium, and Sandalwood.

More crooked than a dog's hind leg.
—Mamaw Betsy

It's hotter than two rats fucking in a wool sock
by a fireplace. —Grammy Sis

You look more nervous than a long-tailed tomcat
in a room full of rocking chairs. —Gramma Angel

STOP PANIC ATTACKS

If you suffer from panic attacks, then you will understand the desperate attempts to rid yourself of the nasty attacks. Most people rush to a psychiatrist to get medicine like antidepressants or benzodiazepines to reduce the severity of panic attacks. Both these drugs may work, but drugs can come with some severe side-effects. Essential oils can help maintain a stable calm, reduce the chance of panic attacks, and give you a healthy and natural way to fight panic attacks.

Using essential oils can calm your nerves and help you fight off panic attacks. It is more helpful to use them before having an attack, as a preventive method. Aromatherapy is a safe and effective way to help keep panic attacks from flaring before they happen.

For those who don't know what exactly a panic attack entails, it is a process where your emotions take over your mental state. You react, panic, and fall into a stage of ultimate panic. You overreact and your body compensates with its adrenal system by releasing adrenaline. Adrenaline is responsible for the muscle tension and increase in heart rate. Your breathing becomes quick and shallow and your body falls into "fight or flight" state as if you are in danger.

If you are susceptible to panic attacks, use aromatherapy in your office, in your home, or even as a mild cologne or perfume to help keep the aroma available throughout the day. In the office, it will help you deal with the stressful actions that could otherwise trigger a panic attack. At home, aromatherapy can help you relax from a hard day of taking care of kids, and it can help you relax when coming home from work.

The following list of essential oils are effective ways to help fight off panic attacks. Use them individually, or together to help eliminate, control, and calm panic attacks when they happen. Combining Frankincense, Lavender, Neroli and Ylang-Ylang can help fight panic attacks and without the use of harmful drugs.

FRANKINCENSE

Frankincense is a major essential oil that is involved with balancing and relaxing your mind and spirit. The exotic plant is found in Africa as a bush with a beautiful fragrance. It is often recognized from religious stories since it has been a prominently soothing plant for many centuries. The deeply relaxing herb is essential for improving your state of mind and relaxing your body.

LAVENDER FRENCH

Lavender French is cultivated in Europe as a powerful essential oil that soothes your mind, relaxes your spirit, and it even plays as a mild antiseptic. It is a popular, soft and mild scent that has a flowery aura. It can help ease your sore aches and pains in the muscles and it can reduce the head tension from a hard day's work.

NEROLI

Neroli is a distilled oil from the bitter Orange tree. The fragrance relaxes your mind and restores energy levels. It can help relieve anger and irritability and restrains powerful emotions.

YLANG-YLANG

Ylang-Ylang is a sensual oil that can follow up from the other oils to help wrap up your relaxation. It is an exotic aroma that uplifts your spirits and brings peace to your busy mind. It also helps put you in a romantic mood and uplifts your overall outlook on life. Use these essential oils alone or in combination to reduce or eliminate panic attacks.

Other essential oils that can fight fear include Peppermint, Helichrysum, Rose, Rosemary, Lemon, Bergamot, Sandalwood, and Basil.

My great-granny predicted my cousins' gender by tying a needle to a string and holding it above my aunt's belly. If it went back and forth it was one gender, and if it went 'round and 'round it was another. She was right both times.
—Mammy Doris

As soon as baby big enough to start rooting around Pawpaw would put the baby on the edge of the bed with a pillow on the floor. He'd sit on the floor and wait until the baby fell onto the pillow. If a baby doesn't fall off the bed before it's a year old, it will die. My elders called it flipping the baby. —Mamaw Honey

AROMATHERAPY FOR PREGNANCY AND BIRTH

Pregnant women are prone to hormonal imbalances that cause stress and anxiety. Aromatherapy can be used to help pregnant women relax and balance their emotions. Small amounts can be placed in bath water or in a vaporizer to inhale the therapeutic scents.

Essential oils have been used for centuries. In biblical times, Frankincense and Myrrh were used as a meditation fragrance. Using essential oils can help soften the aches and pains that come with stress and anxiety. Although the term aromatherapy is now used, it did not become a common term until the 1920s.

The main ingredient in aromatherapy is essential oils. Essential oils are extracted from various plants that offer therapeutic solutions. The extract is removed, distilled, and bottled in pure form. They are potent oils, and they need to be diluted before proper use as an inhalant or cream.

There are various ways to use the essential oils. Before choosing, you should research and study which essential oil is best for your condition. Test the fragrance to make sure there are no allergies. Place a small amount of diluted solution on your skin to make sure that it will not cause any skin irritations.

Place a few drops in a bath and relax your mind and body. Preparing a warm bath and diluting essential oils in the bath can relieve you from mind fatigue. It is incredibly relaxing which is important for an expectant mother. They can also help relieve the aches and pains from your muscles or the tension from the day's events. If you prefer to take a shower, place some droplets behind the drain where the oil can have time to dilute. The warm shower water will dilute the oil leaving an incredibly soothing fragrance.

Although many essential oils have individual benefits, there are also good combinations. Certain combinations of key essential oils can provide a more potent way to treat mental issues and emotional imbalances. They can also help you regain memory and get rid of irritability.

Essential oils are also great for massage. Tiny droplets diluted in massage oils can enhance by relieving tension in muscles and helping soothe sore aches and pains. Use the oils on the temples, forehead, and scalp creates a relaxing effect that removes headaches and leaves your mind refreshed and clear.

Below is a list of essential oils that will help you relax during your pregnancy.

LAVENDER

Lavender is a restoring fragrance that helps relax the mind. It can put you in a euphoric state of rejuvenation and reduce stress. It is also said to strengthen contractions.

CHAMOMILE

This oil is a mild fragrance that calms the mind and the body. It is best for irritability and anxiety. Used in moderation, this fragrance can help you relieve stress and deal with emotional imbalances.

NEROLI

Neroli is an essential oil that helps with depression. It removes the negative thoughts from your mind and helps you relax. It can also help with insomnia and other stress-related illnesses.

BERGAMOT

Bergamot is an effective mood enhancer that also helps you deal with depression. It will clear your mind while the citrus scent uplifts your spirit.

Once you start shaving your legs, there is no going back. —Gee Maw Boo

Milk baths make your skin smooth. Lard or bacon grease is a good substitute for moisturizer. —Gramma Pinky

If you're stuck without blush, flip your head upside-down for a minute so the blood runs to your cheeks. —Granny Harper

Rub olive oil into your hands after a long day of cooking and washing dishes. —Nanny Glessie

HELP WITH POSTPARTUM DEPRESSION

Having a baby is supposed to be a joyous time, but some will suffer postpartum depression. Aromatherapy can help you boost your energy, fight depression, and balance your emotions.

Sometimes postpartum depression stems from hormonal imbalance that cause stress levels to rise.

Environment changes can affect your hormones and mood. The imbalances postpartum can trigger mood swings. Use aromatherapy as a preventive measure, to stimulate body and mind, soothe aches and pains, and clear negative thoughts.

If you are a new mother returning to work, use aromatherapy in the office to help fight against sadness in the office. Using the oils can help provide a better attitude towards customer service. If you are a manager, it will help with human resource and employee issues.

Bergamot, Chamomile, and Neroli are three great essential oils for postpartum depression. Use the oils separately or in combination.

BERGAMOT

Bergamot has a citrus scent which gives the essential oil a powerfully refreshing aura. The citrus smell boosts your energy in the morning and keeps you motivated throughout the day. Its aromatic scent was originally used in colognes and perfumes, and it can be blended with almost any other essential oil.

CHAMOMILE MAROC

Chamomile Maroc is a powerful way to soothe and relax your mind. Combined with Bergamot, Chamomile can help you unwind from the day's busy schedule. It helps balance your emotions so you don't feel like you are losing control. It can help quell anger and irritability.

NEROLI

Neroli is a rejuvenating oil that restores your body and mind's balance. It is a fresh blossom from the Bitter Orange tree that gives this essential oil its health benefits. It will help you get rid of anger and focus on the positive.

ENERGIZE YOURSELF

Essential oils can help you release stress and restore energy levels in your daily active life. Using essential oils in your home, car, office, or any other place can help your energy levels increase, and will leave you feeling vitalized.

Once you choose your essential oil, place a few drops into a burner or on a lightbulb. Another option is to use a diffuser or put some drops into a pendant to smell during the day.

Stress can have a negative effect on your body and inner strength. Aromatherapy helps increase energy levels and hinders high stress.

Your body replenishes levels of energy after sleep, but stress can adversely affect sleep patterns, keeping you tired and agitated during the day. With work pressure, deadlines, and chores, stress can take over your life.

Aromatherapy in the office is especially useful. Probably the most stressful parts of our day involve the office. A few drops in a burner in your office can help reduce stress during a busy work day.

Not all essential oils are strong, pungent smells that travel long distances. Some essential oils are subtle and light. Even at low levels, your body uses them for positive benefits. They can help you relax and increase energy levels even at low levels.

Increasing energy is a major benefit of scents like Grapefruit, Pine Needle, and Litsea Cubeba. Use these essential oil smells separately or in combination for a fully powerful benefit. Each essential oil has a certain effect separately, and in combination are synergistic.

GRAPEFRUIT

If you have ever peeled a fresh grapefruit for a healthy morning breakfast, then you already know the refreshing benefits of Grapefruit. The tangy fruit has an uplifting, stimulating effect from its citrus foundation. Use this oil to invigorate and create a feeling of refreshed energy.

PINE NEEDLE

Having a Christmas Tree inside your home will help you realize the benefits of this aroma. Using this essential oil clears your mind and acts as a refreshing antiseptic. The aroma clears negative thoughts and helps make your body feel revitalized.

LITSEA CUBEBA

A less commonly known essential oil is the Litsea Cubeba. It is an uplifting scent that makes your body feel strengthened and balanced. Like the Grapefruit, it also has a citrus lemon smell that provides a refreshing energy.

Any of the other Citrus oils—Orange, Lemon, Petit grain, Neroli, and Bergamot are great at stimulation and boosting your energy. So are Peppermint and Spearmint.

That's a tough row to hoe, but half a loaf is better than none. I'm going to jerk a knot in your tail. —Meemaw Crone

I like to keep an open mind, but not so open that my brains fall out. Don't believe everything you think. —Meemaw Crone

REJUVENATE YOUR MIND

With all the responsibility and worry that a person needs to juggle, mental fatigue has become common, sapping your energy and mental health. Using aromatherapy will help fight mental fatigue, improving memory, health, and overall mood.

Working life is usually more than the typical eight hours a day. Ten or twelve hour workdays are not uncommon for many people. The fatigue can make you more irritable during the day.

Using aromatherapy will help balance your mood and help you cope with the stress and struggles at work. Burning a few drops during the day in the office will improve your mood almost immediately. You will be able to function better and concentrate. Your stress will drop, allowing you to complete your job with fewer mistakes.

Not all mental fatigue comes from the work environment. Some stress and mental fatigue come from home. A homemaker or stay-at-home mom can also suffer from mental fatigue and stress of keeping schedules, taking care of the kids, and making sure the home is in perfect condition. Use aromatherapy if you feel the day's stress getting the better of you. It can calm your nerves and help balance your emotions.

Using the below essential oils will help revitalize your memory and help remove the mental fatigue. Lavender, Peppermint, and Rosemary help rid your body of stress that creates the mental fatigue. Use the essential oils separately for their individual effects, or in combination for a potent mental fatigue cure.

LAVENDER FRENCH

Lavender French is a relaxing essential oil that protects the mind from fatigue. It is an exotic plant grown in France, that has been used therapeutically for ages. It is used in Europe to relieve tension, soothe aches and pains in the muscles, and help with energy.

PEPPERMINT

Peppermint is a well-known essential oil for its cool scent that revives the senses. The scent penetrates the senses and helps you regain your mental and physical energy. The aromatherapy is especially pleasing after a hard day's work. A few drops will soothe your mind and help you relax for sleep. It also helps relieve aches and pains associated with work.

ROSEMARY

Rosemary is a good essential oil for relieving stress, aches, and pains. Rosemary is said to help your short and long-term memory for concentration and focus on important work.

Use the above essential oils separately or in combination for an effective way to relieve yourself from mental fatigue. A few drops burned during the day will improve your mental health almost immediately.

Sweet oil in the ears for an ear infection.
—Nannie Harper

If you have a fever, put onions slices on your feet (inside your socks). —Big Mama Kate

Put hot rocks (heated by the sun) on itchy poison ivy rashes! —Grandmaw Ida

If we misbehaved at Mawmaw's house, she'd give us a big dose of castor oil. After I was grown I questioned her about this. She laughed and said, "I knew right where y'all'd be the rest of the day. It's hard to get into meanness when you're in the toilet."—Grandma Edie

INCREASE YOUR MEMORY

Our memory is one of the most important functions to maintain. Memory can fade or be inhibited from stress, environment, or sickness. Memory should be exercised to help you increase your ability to retrieve information from long-term memory. While short-term memory only lasts a few seconds, it can also improve.

Aromatherapy may help memory through stimulation. Using essential oils in your home or office will help concentration, revitalize short-term memory, and even help retrieve long-term memory. Memory will help you understand customer needs and help you listen and accommodate your children more effectively.

Using essential oils after work will help you relax and get a better night's sleep, and allow you to wake up refreshed and ready to tackle the day. The relaxing essential oils rest the mind properly at night so it can concentrate more efficiently during the day. Rest stimulates the brain to bring essential nutrients.

Using aromatherapy is also good for the college student. It is hard to juggle classes and homework without suffering from anxiety and low-energy levels. The lost sleep from studying many hours can reduce memory. Using essential oils during the college years can increase your ability to concentrate, study, and remember what you have read. The oils can also help you remember lectures from professors when attending classes.

The following will help you relax and increase memory. They will also help you sleep soundly (one of the best ways to increase your long and short-term memory). Rosemary is the perfect way to help your mind focus and increase your memory, but also take a look at the list at the end.

ROSEMARY

Rosemary is a stimulating essential oil that helps focus and maintain proper concentration to better information retrieval. Burning Rosemary in your home, office, or dorm room can rejuvenate tired muscles and help soothe weary feet.

Using essential oils during the day will help reduce stress and improve focus and concentration. It allows clear thinking while studying or analyzing paperwork. You will also feel sharper and full of energy.

Removing stress from your life helps your memory return. Aromatherapy will help remove stress from your mind and body. Try using a little Rosemary the next time you feel stressed and unable to relax.

Other essential oils known to help with memory include Ginger, Basil, Cypress, Hyssop, Lemon, Peppermint, Grapefruit, Thyme, Black Pepper, and Coriander.

It'll all come out in the wash. —Gram Gram

When someone was tooting their own horn about something minor or worthless, my Guncle said, 'With that and a sharp knife, you can slice bread.'—Auntie Gordon

Always pray about it. —Big Aunty Edie

When things are bad, ask Grandma to garden or cook. She taught me how to bake cornbread and fry chicken. Or we'd eat watermelon outside or break beans on the porch. She would just get my mind off of whatever was bothering me.
—Gram Lily

BETTER YOUR MOOD

Using essential oils is a great way to uplift your mood and put you in good spirits throughout the day. Aromatherapy techniques can be preventive against the stress and low energy that harms your health. Even if you don't expect to have a bad day, essential oils can maintain an uplifted mood when the day starts to go sour. A better mood can make you more productive and customer service oriented. Essential oils can facilitate clear thinking in the office.

Essential oils are also useful in the home for stay at home moms or dads with a hectic schedule. If you find yourself losing your emotional control, use aromatherapy to uplift your mood. The aromatic scents can help you keep positive thoughts, and can even improve concentration.

Using essential oils like Grapefruit, Bergamot, and Geranium can greatly enhance your mood and internal energy levels. The following essential oils can be used individually, but used in combination they provide a powerful way to enhance mood and keep your spirits high.

GRAPEFRUIT

Everyone is familiar with that freshly peeled smell of a ripe grapefruit. The citrus scent immediately makes you feel refreshed and it feels that energy levels instantly rise. The aroma is tangy and brings back an invigorating feeling that happens when your mood quickly becomes better and your spirit is uplifted.

BERGAMOT

Bergamot is an exotic plant extract that is energizing and has an antiseptic for your mind quality. It stimulates your senses and balances emotions while improving mood. The Bergamot aroma is taken from the fruit's peeled layer and was once used in colognes. The Bergamot aroma can be used alone, but also blends well with most other essential oils.

GERANIUM

Geranium is a balancing plant that stabilizes mood and makes you feel spiritually healthier. When you allow stress to enter your life, emotions can affect your health and the people around you. Geranium essential oils can help stabilize emotional imbalance.

Use each of these scents, Grapefruit, Bergamot, and Geranium, individually for their unique emotionally uplifting qualities. Other essential oils known to enhance mood include Lavender,

Frankincense, Lemon, Neroli, Orange, Palo Santo, Rose, Sandalwood, Ylang-Ylang, and Chamomile.

When opportunity knocks, don't sit there complaining about the noise. If you don't sin, Jesus died for nothing. We saddle our own horse where I come from.
—Meemaw Crone

Take all you want, eat all you take. Never hold your farts in. They travel up your spine into your brain, and that's where your crappy ideas come from. —Meemaw Crone

Lord willin' and the creek don't rise, everything
will be just fine. —Meemaw Crone

My grannies were no-nonsense types. One held
a gun under her apron when the civil war
soldiers came by her house. —Nana Earl

Dance 'till the cows come home.
—Meemaw Crone

Good night, sleep tight, and don't let the
bedbugs bite. —Meemaw Crone

My Mama always told us to go to bed with a
clean face (no matter how tired we are), wear
sunscreen under makeup, use moisturizer every
night, and to exercise. —Mammie Aggie

FEEL MORE CONFIDENT

Feelings of insecurity can plague any normal person. The low self-esteem that accompanies insecurity can lead to depression and social anxiety, leading to a downward spiral of negative emotions.

Aromatherapy can help you regain control over negative thoughts, whether caused by anxiety over employment, finances, or relationships.

Essential oils can induce a feeling of happiness, and can help balance emotions when they feel out of control.

Insecurity issues stem from feeling out of control. Long-term relationships that end abruptly, changes at work, violence, or economic downturns result in insecurity.

Frankincense and Sandalwood are two great essential oils to help you prevent depression and fight off insecurities. Use each separately for their individual benefits. Using them in combination creates a powerful solution for depression and anxiety issues.

FRANKINCENSE

Frankincense is a rejuvenating essential oil that will make you feel refreshed and balanced. It is an exotic fragrance that is extracted from special bushes native to Africa. It has been used for thousands of years as a relaxing fragrance and included as part of religious ceremonies. It is also used as an aid in meditation. While relaxing, it also uplifts and improves mood.

SANDALWOOD AGMARK

Sandalwood Agmark is an effectively sensual and soothing essential oil. It helps relax aching muscles and soothes your mind from the anxiety and depression of a hectic day. Coupled with Frankincense, Sandalwood Agmark can aid in relieving your mind from the insecurities that can affect your spirit, body, and mind.

Other essential oils used for confidence include Ylang-Ylang, Bay Laurel, Bergamot, Cypress, Grapefruit, Jasmine, Rosemary, Cedarwood, and Orange.

Additional essential oils for fear include Clary Sage, Lemon, Neroli, Palo Santo, Roman Chamomile, and Vetiver.

SKIN SOLUTIONS—BREAKOUTS AND GROWTHS

Your skin is sensitive to environmental changes, stress, and oily buildup that can lead to breakouts. Some people take medication to fight off acne without knowing their side-effects. Using essential oils is a way to naturally remove acne and keep your skin clear.

Essential oils are non-greasy, so they will not cause a build up and clog your pores. Using essential oils is useful to treat existing acne without using harsh treatments. The list below will help you fight acne, remove blemishes, and tighten small premature wrinkles.

Essential oils are often dissolved in cream or oil and then applied as a moisturizer. Even in small concentrations, they provide medicinal advantages over acne breakouts. The oils bring oxygen and nutrients to the skin, helping it fight off any blemishes. Below is a list of some of the most popular essential oils that will help with your acne treatments.

CLARY SAGE

Clary Sage is extracted from plants that greatly imitate the body's own hormones. The use of Clary Sage is preferred when acne stems from hormonal imbalances. The essential oil can act as a precursor allowing the body to balance its hormones.

EUCALYPTUS

Eucalyptus is a popular plant extract that helps fight off blackheads. It has a cleansing effect that removes dirt and oils and leaves clear skin.

LAVENDER

Lavender is considered an all-purpose oil since its uses include acne treatment and mental fatigue rejuvenation. Lavender is good for the skin, and it can calm your mind and soothe your muscles from stress and anxiety.

LEMON

The citrus impact of Lemon can refresh your mind and restore your skin's natural balance. Lemon oil is known to quickly clear up current acne and remove blemishes. After applying Lemon, one should be careful not to have over-exposure to the sun since it can cause skin discoloration.

MYRRH

Myrrh is a popular, ancient essential oil that was used as a balm to treat sores and scars. Use it to treat rashes and acne breakouts for recurring. Myrrh has many uses including the elimination of warts or acne-causing bacteria.

PATCHOULI

Patchouli is a good essential oil to fight off many skin conditions. It will help you fight off acne, but it is also a good way to treat rashes and scarring. Use it as a moisturizer for its calming fragrance.

Before hosting or attending parties, lie in bed for a half hour with witch-hazel-soaked cotton balls on your eyelids, and look bright-eyed and fresh.
—Grandma Tella

The women in my family aren't big on beautifying, but they love the color red. In old color photos, eight out of ten are wearing red.
—Mamie

On the outside as on the inside. —Ma Patsy

SKIN SOLUTIONS—WARTS, MOLES, & SKIN TAGS

Essential oils known to help with warts, moles, and skin tags include Lavender, Oregano, Frankincense, Melissa, Clove, Myrrh, and Elemi.

In this unique context, essential oils may be used undiluted on skin to burn away growths. Apply sparingly only on the growth. Protect good skin surrounding the application of essential oils with heavy oil or Vaseline.

Don't start anything on Saturday you can't finish. —Meemaw Crone

Red lipstick on a date tells a man you're ready to play in the hay. —Bunnie Gam Gam

I'm not as young as a spring chicken anymore. Once burned, twice learned. —Meemaw Crone

SKIN SOLUTIONS—ANTI-AGING

Carrier oils come into play when seeking an anti-aging regimen. Use a combination of Primrose Seed, Rosehip Seed, Pomegranate Seed, Apricot Kernel, and Jojoba.

Add these essential oils to the mix—Carrot, Frankincense, Cypress, Myrrh, and Rosemary.

Carrier oils will plump and rejuvenate your skin, and the essential oils with promote tautness, cell regeneration, and reduce spider veins and wrinkles.

Use the coupon code FIVE%OFF for 5% off your order of Kentucky Crone products at www.kentuckycrone.com. (Products bought on Amazon.com are not included in this offer.)

Well hush my puppies, I'm done.
—Meemaw Crone